CNN 10, Vol. 2
– Student News –

NEWS EXPLAINED IN 10 MINUTES

by
Fuyuhiko Sekido
Masato Kogure
Jake Arnold
Christopher Mattson
Kazushige Cho

Asahi Press

《《《 音声ストリーミング・ダウンロード配信 》》》

http://text.asahipress.com/free/english/

この教科書の音声は、上記ウェブサイトにて無料で配信しています。

CNN 10, Vol. 2
Copyright © 2019 by Asahi Press

All rights reserved. No part of this book may be reproduced or transmitted in any form or by any means, electronic or mechanical, including photocopying, recording or by any information storage and retrieval system, without permission in writing from the authors and the publisher.

は　し　が　き

　このテキストはアメリカの学生向けニュース番組 CNN 10 (旧 CNN Student News) を用いて日本の学習者、主に大学生のみなさんが英語を学習しやすいように編集、執筆されたテキストです。CNN Student News vol.1 から数えると通算で 7 冊目となります。実際の番組 CNN 10 では、毎回 10 分間アメリカの学期に合わせて土日を除くほぼ毎日放送され、Web 上でも配信されています。本テキストではそれらの中から約 2～3 分で完結しているニュースを選び教材化しました。内容は執筆者たちがバラエティに富むようにと心がけ、様々なジャンルから選んでいます。また、英語自体も難しすぎないものを選んだので、英語があまり得意でない学習者でも学ぶことができるように努めました。Unit は全部で 15 Units あるので、担当の先生の方針によっては 1 回の授業に 1 Unit で半期に、あるいは 2 回の授業に 1 Unit を用いて通年で学んでいく可能性があります。各 Unit は内容は違うものの、学習していく順序・項目は同じような構成になっています。詳しくは本書の使い方を参照してください。授業内外にての予習・復習などに関しては先生の指示に従ってください。

　このテキストを通して、みなさんが CNN 10、そして英語とニュースに関心を持ち、楽しみながら学習していけることを願っています。

CNN 10 の特徴

　CNN 10 はそのタイトル通り、CNN が発信している 10 分間のニュース番組です。10 分間という短い時間であってもニュースの内容は様々で、時には日本のニュースも登場しています。番組ではアンカーと呼ばれる司会者 Carl Azuz (アズーズ) が最初のニュースを紹介し、その後小さな 1～2 分のニュースがいくつか紹介されますが、テーマによっては長めのものもあります。なお、内容を理解するための知識をクイズ形式で紹介しており、番組自体に若干エンターテインメント的な要素も含まれています。過去のニュースはアーカイブ形式で保存されているので、数ヶ月前のニュースを見ることも可能です。さらに、番組の Web 上にはニュースで話された英語がスクリプトとしてあるので、文字として確認しながら音声を聞けます。よって本テキストで学習した後、さらにニュースを見て同じような学習を継続して行いたい場合、みなさんご自身の興味に従って自発的にそれらを用いて学習していくことも出来ますので、以下の URL から一度 Web にアクセスしてみてください。

http://edition.cnn.com/cnn10/

　本テキスト執筆にあたり、朝日英一郎氏をはじめ、朝日出版社のスタッフの方々に多大なるご支援、ご協力をいただきました。この場を借りて、御礼申し上げます。

著者一同

本書の使い方

Warm up
Unitのトピックを学んでいくにあたり、関連するスモールトークの練習ができます。ペアやグループで話し合ったり、1人でライティングの練習もできます。

Vocabulary Exercise
先のVocabularyのセクションで学んだ単語を、別の例文の中で用いてみる練習です。例文ごと覚えてしまいましょう。同じ単語は一度しか用いませんので、やや難しく感じる方々でもわかるものからやっていけば消去法ですべて選択していくことが出来ます。積極的に取り組んで下さい。また3 Unitsごとに、"Vocabulary / Idioms in the News"と題したドリルを設けました。前3 Unitsに出てきた表現を特集しています。

Topic Paragraph
ニュースを理解していくにあたり、まずは導入の部分のみ音声や動画を用いて確認します。発音や音読の練習をしながらTrue/False Questionsもやってみましょう。

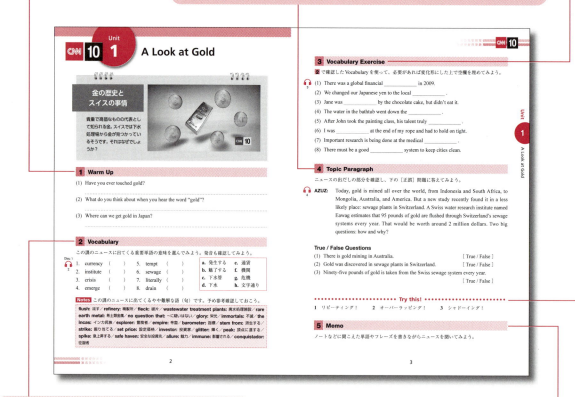

Vocabulary
ニュースを理解するための重要な単語を選んであります。基本単語なので意味や発音を確実に確認しましょう。さらに難しい単語や表現は、Notesにまとめてありますので、必要に応じて参照してください。

Memo
ニュースをとりあえず一度聞いてみて、残りの部分がどのくらい理解できるのか、試してみるためにMemoのコーナーを作りました。音声を聞くだけでも、あるいは動画を見ながらでも、どちらでもかまわないので先生の指示に従いながら取り組んでください。メモを取り終わったら、どんな内容や単語を聞き取れたのか、ペアやグループで確認してみるとよいでしょう。

音声は放送そのままのオリジナル放送音源と、それをスタジオでゆっくりとしたスピードで読み直したスロースピード音源の2種類を用意してありますので、生のニュースを聴き取る練習に最適です。

Transcript Completion

リスニングのセクションです。本文中に空欄が10〜15箇所前後ありますので、リスニング力を確認してください。

Comprehension Questions

True/False Questions（正誤問題）です。ニュースをTopic Paragraph の後、大まかに3箇所に区切り、その区切りごとに問題を付しました。ニュース全体を聞いてからでは内容を把握しきれないことも考えて、このような配慮を施しました。

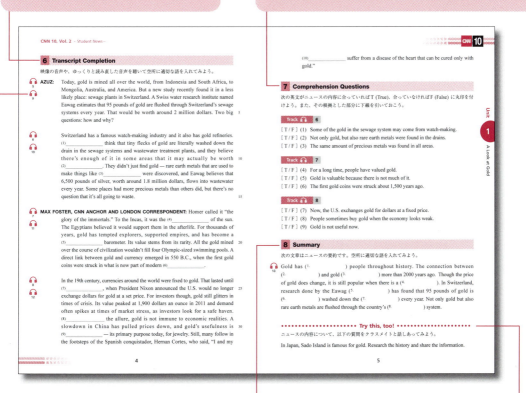

Summary

本テキスト執筆者による、オリジナル英文でのニュースの要約です。そこに空欄を設けてありますので、これを埋めることでニュースの理解が促進されます。ここはリスニングとして音声を聞きながら、あるいはあえて聞かないで理解を試す、のどちらでも利用出来ますので先生の指示に従ってください。また、空欄に用いる単語はVocabularyのセクションで用いたものなので、語彙の復習としても用いることが出来ます。

Try this, too!

Unit 最後の活動はニュースの内容についての意見交換です。質問に答えるように、あるいはその質問をきっかけにしてさらなる意見などが出てくるとよいでしょう。うまく話せないと感じたら、前もって意見を英語、もしくは日本語で、メモしておいて、それからチャレンジしてみてください。また、意見交換のあと、さらにどう思ったかをライティングの形でまとめてみるなども英語を発信するよい練習かもしれません。

Try this!

Topic Paragraph を実際に声に出して読んでみましょう。最初は音声を聞き、一定の長さに区切った部分を同じように発音してみます。これをリピーティングと言います。次に、音声に合わせて、出来ればなるべく遅れないように、発音とリズム、イントネーションなどをまねしながら読みます。これがオーバーラッピングです。最後に、スクリプトを見ずに、音声だけを頼りにして、若干遅れてもいいのでなるべくついていって一緒に読みます。これがシャドーイングです。先生の指示に従いながら、積極的に練習してみてください。

Contents
CNN 10, Vol. 2 – Student News –

はしがき
本書の使い方

Unit 1	**A Look at Gold** ……………………………………………… 2
	— 金の歴史とスイスの事情 —

Unit 2	**Daylight Savings** ……………………………………… 6
	— 標準時間と夏時間 —

Unit 3	**Making Libraries** ……………………………………… 10
	— 図書館を作ろう —

Unit 4	**Pyramid Tech** …………………………………………… 16
	— ピラミッドとテクノロジー —

Unit 5	**Pigments** ………………………………………………………… 20
	— 不思議な顔料 —

Unit 6	**Shopping Tech** ………………………………………… 26
	— 未来型ショッピング —

Unit 7	**Origami** …………………………………………………………… 32
	— 科学者で折り紙職人 —

Unit 8	**Ice Cream** ……………………………………………………… 38
	— アイスクリーム大学 —

Unit 9	**Nigerian Women's Bobsled Team** ⋯⋯⋯ 44 ― ナイジェリア出身の女性ボブスレー選手 ―	
Unit 10	**Zoo Dog** ⋯⋯⋯⋯⋯⋯⋯⋯⋯⋯⋯⋯⋯⋯⋯ 50 ― 動物を管轄する動物 ―	
Unit 11	**Google Before Google** ⋯⋯⋯⋯⋯⋯⋯ 54 ― グーグルがなかった時代には ―	
Unit 12	**3D Food Printing** ⋯⋯⋯⋯⋯⋯⋯⋯⋯ 58 ― 料理を3Dプリンターで ―	
Unit 13	**Bitcoin** ⋯⋯⋯⋯⋯⋯⋯⋯⋯⋯⋯⋯⋯⋯⋯ 64 ― ビットコインのオモテとウラ ―	
Unit 14	**Money to Soil** ⋯⋯⋯⋯⋯⋯⋯⋯⋯⋯⋯ 70 ― 古くなった紙幣は土へ ―	
Unit 15	**Net Neutrality** ⋯⋯⋯⋯⋯⋯⋯⋯⋯⋯⋯ 76 ― ネットワーク中立性を考えよう ―	

Vocabulary / Idioms in the News ⋯⋯⋯⋯ 15, 31, 49, 63, 81

Unit 1 A Look at Gold

金の歴史とスイスの事情

貴重で高価なものの代表として知られる金。スイスでは下水処理場から金が見つかっているそうです。それはなぜでしょうか？

1 Warm Up

(1) Have you ever touched gold?

(2) What do you think about when you hear the word "gold"?

(3) Where can we get gold in Japan?

2 Vocabulary

この課のニュースに出てくる重要単語の意味を選んでみよう。発音も確認してみよう。

Disc 1 / 2

1. currency (　)
2. institute (　)
3. crisis (　)
4. emerge (　)
5. tempt (　)
6. sewage (　)
7. literally (　)
8. drain (　)

a. 発生する　e. 通貨
b. 魅了する　f. 機関
c. 下水管　　g. 危機
d. 下水　　　h. 文字通り

Notes この課のニュースに出てくるやや難解な語（句）です。予め参考確認しておこう。

flush: 流す／**refinery:** 精製所／**fleck:** 破片／**wastewater treatment plants:** 廃水処理施設／**rare earth metal:** 希土類金属／**no question that:** 〜に疑いはない／**glory:** 栄光／**immortals:** 不滅／**the Incas:** インカ民族／**explorer:** 冒険者／**empire:** 帝国／**barometer:** 指標／**stem from:** 派生する／**strike:** 掘り当てる／**set price:** 設定価格／**investor:** 投資家／**glitter:** 輝く／**peak:** 頂点に達する／**spike:** 急上昇する／**safe haven:** 安全な投資先／**allure:** 魅力／**immune:** 影響される／**conquistador:** 征服者

3 Vocabulary Exercise

2 で確認した Vocabulary を使って、必要があれば変化形にした上で空欄を埋めてみよう。

(1) There was a global financial _____ in 2009.
(2) We changed our Japanese yen to the local _____ .
(3) Jane was _____ by the chocolate cake, but didn't eat it.
(4) The water in the bathtub went down the _____ .
(5) After John took the painting class, his talent truly _____ .
(6) I was _____ at the end of my rope and had to hold on tight.
(7) Important research is being done at the medical _____ .
(8) There must be a good _____ system to keep cities clean.

4 Topic Paragraph

ニュースの出だしの部分を確認し、下の［正誤］問題に答えてみよう。

AZUZ: Today, gold is mined all over the world, from Indonesia and South Africa, to Mongolia, Australia, and America. But a new study recently found it in a less likely place: sewage plants in Switzerland. A Swiss water research institute named Eawag estimates that 95 pounds of gold are flushed through Switzerland's sewage systems every year. That would be worth around 2 million dollars. Two big questions: how and why?

True / False Questions
(1) There is gold mining in Australia.　　　　　　　　　　　［ True / False ］
(2) Gold was discovered in sewage plants in Switzerland.　　［ True / False ］
(3) Ninety-five pounds of gold is taken from the Swiss sewage system every year.
　　　　　　　　　　　　　　　　　　　　　　　　　　　　［ True / False ］

•••••••••••••••••••••• **Try this!** ••••••••••••••••••••••
1　リピーティング！　　2　オーバーラッピング！　　3　シャドーイング！

5 Memo

ノートなどに聞こえた単語やフレーズを書きながらニュースを聞いてみよう。

6 Transcript Completion

映像の音声や、ゆっくりと読み直した音声を聴いて空所に適切な語を入れてみよう。

AZUZ: Today, gold is mined all over the world, from Indonesia and South Africa, to Mongolia, Australia, and America. But a new study recently found it in a less likely place: sewage plants in Switzerland. A Swiss water research institute named Eawag estimates that 95 pounds of gold are flushed through Switzerland's sewage systems every year. That would be worth around 2 million dollars. Two big questions: how and why?

Switzerland has a famous watch-making industry and it also has gold refineries. (1)_____ think that tiny flecks of gold are literally washed down the drain in the sewage systems and wastewater treatment plants, and they believe there's enough of it in some areas that it may actually be worth (2)_____. They didn't just find gold — rare earth metals that are used to make things like (3)_____ were discovered, and Eawag believes that 6,500 pounds of silver, worth around 1.8 million dollars, flows into wastewater every year. Some places had more precious metals than others did, but there's no question that it's all going to waste.

MAX FOSTER, CNN ANCHOR AND LONDON CORRESPONDENT: Homer called it "the glory of the immortals." To the Incas, it was the (4)_____ of the sun. The Egyptians believed it would support them in the afterlife. For thousands of years, gold has tempted explorers, supported empires, and has become a (5)_____ barometer. Its value stems from its rarity. All the gold mined over the course of civilization wouldn't fill four Olympic-sized swimming pools. A direct link between gold and currency emerged in 550 B.C., when the first gold coins were struck in what is now part of modern (6)_____.

In the 19th century, currencies around the world were fixed to gold. That lasted until (7)_____, when President Nixon announced the U.S. would no longer exchange dollars for gold at a set price. For investors though, gold still glitters in times of crisis. Its value peaked at 1,900 dollars an ounce in 2011 and demand often spikes at times of market stress, as investors look for a safe haven. (8)_____ the allure, gold is not immune to economic realities. A slowdown in China has pulled prices down, and gold's usefulness is (9)_____ — its primary purpose today, for jewelry. Still, many follow in the footsteps of the Spanish conquistador, Hernan Cortes, who said, "I and my

(10)_____ suffer from a disease of the heart that can be cured only with gold."

7 Comprehension Questions

次の英文がニュースの内容に合っていればT (True)、合っていなければF (False) に丸印を付けよう。また、その根拠とした部分に下線を引いておこう。

Track 6

[T / F]　(1)　Some of the gold in the sewage system may come from watch-making.
[T / F]　(2)　Not only gold, but also rare earth metals were found in the drains.
[T / F]　(3)　The same amount of precious metals was found in all areas.

Track 7

[T / F]　(4)　For a long time, people have valued gold.
[T / F]　(5)　Gold is valuable because there is not much of it.
[T / F]　(6)　The first gold coins were struck about 1,500 years ago.

Track 8

[T / F]　(7)　Now, the U.S. exchanges gold for dollars at a fixed price.
[T / F]　(8)　People sometimes buy gold when the economy looks weak.
[T / F]　(9)　Gold is not useful now.

8 Summary

次の文章はニュースの要約です。空所に適切な語を入れてみよう。

Gold has (1._____) people throughout history. The connection between (2._____) and gold (3._____) more than 2000 years ago. Though the price of gold does change, it is still popular when there is a (4._____). In Switzerland, research done by the Eawag (5._____) has found that 95 pounds of gold is (6._____) washed down the (7._____) every year. Not only gold but also rare earth metals are flushed through the country's (8._____) system.

●●●●●●●●●●●●●●●●●●● **Try this, too!** ●●●●●●●●●●●●●●●●●●●

ニュースの内容について、以下の質問をクラスメイトと話しあってみよう。

In Japan, Sado Island is famous for gold. Research the history and share the information.

Unit 2 Daylight Savings

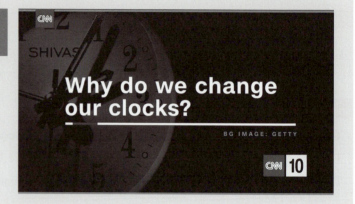

標準時間と夏時間

季節によって時間を少し動かす国もあります。その理由と歴史、現状についてのレポートを見てみましょう。

1 Warm Up

(1) Do you know when the sunrise and sunset are in your city now?

(2) If you had an extra hour of time every day, what would you do?

(3) What is the best part of the day?

2 Vocabulary

この課のニュースに出てくる重要単語の意味を選んでみよう。発音も確認してみよう。

1. region   (　)   5. observe   (　)
2. consumption (　)   6. extend   (　)
3. notable   (　)   7. assume   (　)
4. election   (　)   8. voter   (　)

a. 順守する   e. 伸びる
b. 明らかな   f. 仮定する
c. 選挙   g. 投票者
d. 地域   h. 消費

Notes この課のニュースに出てくるやや難解な語（句）です。予め参考確認しておこう。

folks: 人々／**fall back to:** 〜に戻る／**standard time:** 標準時間／**technically:** 技術的に／**be supposed to:** 〜になる／**spring** (v): 跳ねる（ここでは春の意味のspringと時間が「跳ねる」（時計を進める）をかけたシャレ。アメリカでは夏時間の切り替え時に時計をセットする際 "spring ahead, fall back" という）／**the Standard Time Act:** 標準時間法／**trick-or-treaters:** ハロウィンでお菓子をもらうために家々を回る子どもたち／**voter turnout:** 投票率／**smoke detector:** 煙感知器

3 Vocabulary Exercise

2 で確認した Vocabulary を使って、必要があれば変化形にした上で空欄を埋めてみよう。

(1) The monkey _____ his arm to reach the fruit.
(2) Because he was late, Jane _____ Harry wouldn't come.
(3) The _____ of sugar by Japanese people went up last year.
(4) Hundreds of _____ lined up at the community center on election day.
(5) Because she practices every day, Kaho has made _____ progress.
(6) The _____ is famous for its mountains and thick forests.
(7) The townspeople _____ the strict traffic laws, so most people drive carefully.
(8) Today is an _____ day, when people can vote for their favorite politician.

4 Topic Paragraph

ニュースの出だしの部分を確認し、下の［正誤］問題に答えてみよう。

AZUZ: If you live in the U.S. or Canada, you could get an extra hour of sleep this Saturday night, assuming you don't stay up later than usual. Folks in the region will be falling back to standard time. That's what it's called when it's no longer Daylight Saving Time and technically, at 2 o'clock a.m. Sunday, we're supposed to set our clocks back to 1 a.m. Why do we do this?

True / False Questions

(1) People can sleep longer than usual this Saturday night.　　　[True / False]
(2) Daylight Saving Time is one hour behind standard time.　　　[True / False]
(3) People should set their clocks back at 2 o'clock a.m. Sunday.　　　[True / False]

• **Try this!** •

1　リピーティング！　　2　オーバーラッピング！　　3　シャドーイング！

5 Memo

ノートなどに聞こえた単語やフレーズを書きながらニュースを聞いてみよう。

6 Transcript Completion

映像の音声や、ゆっくりと読み直した音声を聴いて空所に適切な語を入れてみよう。

AZUZ: If you live in the U.S. or Canada, you could get an extra hour of sleep this Saturday night, assuming you don't stay up later than usual. Folks in the region will be falling back to standard time. That's what it's called when it's no longer Daylight Saving Time and technically, at 2 o'clock a.m. Sunday, we're supposed to set our clocks back to 1 a.m. Why do we do this?

JENNIFER GRAY, AMS METEOROLOGIST: So why do we change the clocks ahead one hour in the spring and back one hour in the fall? Well, it's actually to (1)_____ the electricity consumption by extending the daylight hours.

GRAY: In the U.S., we change our clocks at 2 a.m. on the second Sunday in (2)_____. That begins Daylight Saving Time, that's when we spring ahead. On the first Sunday in (3)_____, we change our clocks to 2 a.m. again, that's actually just going back to standard time.

(4)_____ it or (5)_____, this started with an idea from Benjamin Franklin. Franklin did write an essay suggesting that people could use less candles if they got up early and made better use of daylight. In (6)_____, the Standard Time Act established time zones, and Daylight Saving Time. But not all states participate. To this day, most of Arizona and all of (7)_____ do not change their clocks. Over 70 countries across the world observe Daylight Saving Time, with notable exceptions of (8)_____ and (9)_____.

In 2007, we actually changed the date of when we set our clocks back an hour to the first week in November. This helped (10)_____ trick-or-treaters by giving them an extra hour of daylight. One of the other lines of thinking was that we would have a better voter turnout on election years. (11)_____ say each time you change your clocks, it's always a good idea to change those batteries in your smoke detector and always look forward to fall when you get that extra hour of (12)_____.

7 Comprehension Questions

次の英文がニュースの内容に合っていればT (True)、合っていなければF (False) に丸印を付けよう。また、その根拠とした部分に下線を引いておこう。

Track 18

[T / F] (1) Daylight Saving Time was created to save electricity.
[T / F] (2) March is when standard time starts.
[T / F] (3) Daylight Saving Time lasts for half a year.

Track 19

[T / F] (4) Benjamin Franklin created Daylight Saving Time.
[T / F] (5) Every state sets their clocks back in November.
[T / F] (6) The U.S. is not the only country to put clocks forward in spring.

Track 20

[T / F] (7) Changing the date to set the clocks back was for kids' safety.
[T / F] (8) Some people think that more people vote during Daylight Saving Time.
[T / F] (9) We can get more sleep in autumn because of this system.

8 Summary

次の文章はニュースの要約です。空所に適切な語を入れてみよう。

Almost all (1.　　　　　) of the U.S. and Canada, except Hawaii and most of Arizona, (2.　　　　　) Daylight Saving Time. Outside of North America, another 70 countries participate in this system, though it is (3.　　　　　) that China and Japan do not. Daylight Saving Time (4.　　　　　) the hours of daylight and was introduced to reduce the (5.　　　　　) of power. In addition, some people also think that more (6.　　　　　) will vote in (7.　　　　　) if the system is used. When clocks return to standard time, (8.　　　　　) people don't stay up late, they get an extra hour of sleep!

•   **Try this, too!**   •

ニュースの内容について、以下の質問をクラスメイトと話しあってみよう。

Discuss the advantages and disadvantages of introducing Daylight Saving Time in Japan. If introduced, what would happen?

Unit 3 Making Libraries

図書館を作ろう

本を借りたい時に利用する図書館。図書館が与えてくれる喜びと、地域に図書館を作ろうとしている人々の声を、聞いてみましょう。

1 Warm Up

(1) How often do you use the library?

(2) If you were the owner of a library, what kind of books would you get for your library?

(3) Tell your partner about your favorite book.

2 Vocabulary

この課のニュースに出てくる重要単語の意味を選んでみよう。発音も確認してみよう。

26

1. donor   (   )   5. nurture   (   )
2. transform   (   )   6. literacy   (   )
3. awesome   (   )   7. outdated   (   )
4. fund (v)   (   )   8. bother   (   )

a. 素敵な   e. 寄付者
b. 成長させる   f. 時代遅れの
c. 読み書き能力 g. 変える
d. 困惑させる   h. 資金援助を与える

Notes この課のニュースに出てくるやや難解な語（句）です。予め参考確認しておこう。

promote: 推進する／**Ph.D.:** 博士号／**doctorate:** 博士の学位／**have room for:** 〜にスペースがある／**underserved:** 十分なサービスを受けられない／**rely on:** 頼りにする／**catalogue** (v): 目録を作成する／**be reflective of:** 〜を反映する／**before you know it:** いつの間にか／**navigate:** うまく運ぶ／**core:** 中心

3 Vocabulary Exercise

2 で確認した Vocabulary を使って、必要があれば変化形にした上で空欄を埋めてみよう。

(1) Mrs. Lee is older, so sometimes she uses _____ expressions.
(2) Have you seen the new samurai movie? It's _____!
(3) Many different people and organizations _____ the children's art project.
(4) It _____ me when people drive too fast in my neighborhood.
(5) Young children should learn to read to improve their _____ skills.
(6) The _____ gave money and food to help homeless people.
(7) Animals born in zoos should be carefully _____ when they are babies.
(8) Students planted trees in the park and _____ it into a green space.

4 Topic Paragraph

ニュースの出だしの部分を確認し、下の［正誤］問題に答えてみよう。

AZUZ: It makes sense that Rebecca Constantino would work to promote language, literacy and learning — she has a Ph.D. in that. And shortly after she got her doctorate in 1999, she saw something that bothered her in a wealthy part of Los Angeles, California. She says a school was getting rid of its books because it didn't have room for them in the library. So, Constantino took those books to a school in a poorer part of the city and that was the start of Access Books.

True / False Questions

(1) Rebecca Constantino studied literacy. [True / False]
(2) A school in Los Angeles had too many books for their library. [True / False]
(3) Constantino bought books for a school in a poorer area. [True / False]

• **Try this!** •

1 リピーティング！   2 オーバーラッピング！   3 シャドーイング！

5 Memo

ノートなどに聞こえた単語やフレーズを書きながらニュースを聞いてみよう。

6 Transcript Completion

映像の音声や、ゆっくりと読み直した音声を聴いて空所に適切な語を入れてみよう。

AZUZ: It makes sense that Rebecca Constantino would work to promote language, literacy and learning — she has a Ph.D. in that. And shortly after she got her doctorate in 1999, she saw something that bothered her in a wealthy part of Los Angeles, California. She says a school was getting rid of its books because it didn't have room for them in the library. So, Constantino took those books to a school in a poorer part of the city and that was the start of Access Books.

REBECCA CONSTANTINO, CNN HERO: For a child, the library can be a (1)_____ place.

UNIDENTIFIED GIRL: I'm officially the most awesome girl in the world.

CONSTANTINO: It can transform you academically, but it can also nurture you (2)_____. I'm excited. This is going to be our nicest library by far. What people don't realize is that school libraries are sometimes not funded at all.

UNIDENTIFIED FEMALE: It will be full of books over here.

CONSTANTINO: This (3)_____ in schools with outdated collections, books from the 50's, sometimes even the 30's. This only happens because we all work together.

We provide libraries for underserved communities and schools. Our whole goal is to spread literacy and the (4)_____ of literacy. We rely on two groups. We rely on donors and with that donor money, we buy brand new, high interest books and we catalogue them ourselves, so the cost is very (5)_____. It's about 70 percent off list price. And then we rely on volunteers to give gently used donated books. We don't just come in and give you books. So, you ready? The (6)_____ comes to help and the kids come and help. We paint murals in the library that are reflective of what the school wants and books that they've read. So, it's really (7)_____ and welcoming. We really transform it. When kids come back and they see their library, they're completely (8)_____ at how beautiful the space looks, and they really get this sense that wow, I'm important. And this space is important.

UNIDENTIFIED FEMALE: Three to four thousand books came in. So, that's life changing. That's just a (9)_____ experience for the students.

UNIDENTIFIED GIRL: You're clearly a genius.

CONSTANTINO: We've helped over (10)_____ libraries...

GROUP: Yay, books!

CONSTANTINO: ...and we've done (11)_____ community libraries, which means they're at a homeless shelter or a battered woman's shelter. We've distributed over one and a half million books. I want kids to love reading. Reading opens up a whole new world. You learn (12)_____. You learn to problem-solve. And before you know it, you know how to navigate things in life. Really the core of it all is books.

GROUP: Read!

7 Comprehension Questions

次の英文がニュースの内容に合っていればT (True)、合っていなければF (False)に丸印を付けよう。また、その根拠とした部分に下線を引いておこう。

Track 30

[T / F] (1) Libraries can help a child to grow emotionally.

[T / F] (2) All school libraries are funded.

[T / F] (3) Some school libraries have very old books.

Track 31

[T / F] (4) Access Books uses money from donations to buy books.

[T / F] (5) All of the books donated are new.

[T / F] (6) The murals make the children feel good about their library.

Track 32

[T / F] (7) Constantino only donates to school libraries.

[T / F] (8) She has bought more than one and a half million books.

[T / F] (9) Books help people have a better life.

8 Summary

次の文章はニュースの要約です。空所に適切な語を入れてみよう。

Rebecca Constantino was (1.   ) by the fact that some schools have too many books, while others have libraries that are not (2.   ) at all. Those libraries may have only very (3.   ) books. Constantino believes that (4.   ) libraries can help to emotionally (5.   ) children, so she set up Access Books, an organization which creates new libraries or (6.   ) existing ones. In order to positively affect (7.   ) in this way, Access Books relies on (8.   ) and volunteers to provide money, books, and time.

• **Try this, too!** •

ニュースの内容について、以下の質問をクラスメイトと話しあってみよう。

Libraries are important! Imagine you are the librarian of your school. Think of some ideas to encourage students to read and present your ideas to your classmates.

Vocabulary / Idioms in the News
From Units 1-3

ここでは上記Unitに出てきた表現を特集して学習できます。

Exercise

左側の英単語・語句の意味を、右側の日本語訳と正しくつなげてみよう。

1.	stem from	( )	a.	いつの間にか
2.	follow in the footsteps	( )	b.	有効活用する
3.	in times of (crisis)	( )	c.	派生する
4.	by far	( )	d.	スペースがある
5.	before you know it	( )	e.	（全く新しい）世界を開く
6.	have room for	( )	f.	これまでのところ
7.	open up a (whole new) world	( )	g.	（危機）の時に
8.	believe it or not	( )	h.	足跡をたどる
9.	make better use of	( )	i.	考え方
10.	line of thinking	( )	j.	信じられないような話ですが

Unit 4 Pyramid Tech

ピラミッドとテクノロジー

ピラミッドは何千年にも亘る人類の歴史の証でもあります。現代の科学技術はその保存と復元にどのくらい成功しているのでしょうか？

1 Warm Up

(1) Do you know how the pyramids in Egypt were built?

(2) What is a pyramid? Can you explain in English?

(3) Why do you think the Egyptian pyramids have lasted this long?

2 Vocabulary

この課のニュースに出てくる重要単語の意味を選んでみよう。発音も確認してみよう。

1. assemble   (   )
2. vivid   (   )
3. replica   (   )
4. philosophy (   )
5. tomb   (   )
6. flexible   (   )
7. astonishing (   )
8. obsession (   )

a. 哲学　　　e. 驚異的な
b. レプリカ　f. まばゆい
c. こだわり　g. 組み立てる
d. 墓　　　　h. 柔らかい

Notes この課のニュースに出てくるやや難解な語（句）です。予め参考確認しておこう。

document (v): 記録する／**pharaoh**: ファラオ／**Seti I**: セティ1世（古代エジプト第19王朝の第2代ファラオ）／**articulate**: 明確な／**Egyptologists**: エジプト学者／**facsimile**: 複製／**precise recreation**: 正確な再現／**molds**: 型／**operation**: 作業／**mill**: 平削り盤にかける／**frescos**: フレスコ画／**the Great Belzoni**: 偉人ベルツオーニ／**entrance**: 引きつける／**hack off**: 切り取る／**fragment**: 断片／**end up**: 結局～になる／**relief**: レリーフ（浮き彫り）彫刻／**Goddess Maat**: 女神マアト／**feather headdress**: 羽毛の頭飾り／**protective**: 保護の

3 Vocabulary Exercise

2 で確認した Vocabulary を使って、必要があれば変化形にした上で空欄を埋めてみよう。

(1) The painting's colors were really _____ and bright.

(2) Haruka's _____ is collecting old comic books.

(3) Gymnasts must have very _____ bodies to be successful.

(4) A _____ is the way you look at and experience the world.

(5) The fireworks display was _____ to everyone there.

(6) Tony bought the desk at the furniture store and _____ it himself at home.

(7) The family _____ held the bones of many kings and queens.

(8) Instead of buying a real sword, he bought a very good _____ .

4 Topic Paragraph

ニュースの出だしの部分を確認し、下の［正誤］問題に答えてみよう。

UNIDENTIFIED MALE: The magic is seeing this with candlelight.

REPORTER: Adam Lowe freely admits that he is a man with an obsession — to document the tomb of an ancient Egyptian pharaoh, Seti I.

True / False Questions

(1) The tomb looks amazing in the light from a candle.　　［ True / False ］

(2) Adam Lowe keeps his obsession a secret.　　［ True / False ］

(3) The tomb of Seti I is very interesting to Adam Lowe.　　［ True / False ］

・・・・・・・・・・・・・・・・・・・ **Try this!** ・・・・・・・・・・・・・・・・・・・

1　リピーティング！　　2　オーバーラッピング！　　3　シャドーイング！

5 Memo

ノートなどに聞こえた単語やフレーズを書きながらニュースを聞いてみよう。

6 Transcript Completion

映像の音声や、ゆっくりと読み直した音声を聴いて空所に適切な語を入れてみよう。

UNIDENTIFIED MALE: The magic is seeing this with candlelight.

REPORTER: Adam Lowe freely admits that he is a man with an obsession — to document the tomb of an ancient Egyptian pharaoh, Seti I.

UNIDENTIFIED MALE: The tomb actually tells us how the people from three and a half thousand years ago think different things, have different (1)_____, value different things. The way they thought can be read through the very articulate (2)_____ that's on the walls of these tombs. And if we can really build a dialogue that crosses time and use technology to help that, I think we're at an (3)_____ exciting moment.

REPORTER: Just a room you think, but what a room. Known among Egyptologists as "The Hall of Beauties." What's just as astonishing is that this is in fact a facsimile, a precise recreation in a museum in Switzerland of how the room looked exactly 200 years ago when the tomb was (4)_____. Adam Lowe's specialist art company, Factum Arte, has made tomb facsimiles before. They scanned the tomb of Tutankhamun in (5)_____ and made a replica now installed as a tourist (6)_____ in Egypt. The same methods were used for Seti's tomb.

UNIDENTIFIED MALE: We're now making high resolution molds using 3D printing technologies, from laser scan datas that have never involved any contact with the wall.

REPORTER: No contact at all?

UNIDENTIFIED MALE: Zero contact at any point in any of the (7)_____.

REPORTER: The Seti replica was milled in the Factum Arte workshop in Madrid, and a fine flexible (8)_____ added with a printout of the frescos. The facsimile was assembled in panels. Seti's tomb was discovered in 1817 by an Italian circus strongman, an adventurer known as the Great Belzoni. The vivid decoration entranced him. And as a (9)_____, a series of watercolors was painted. But soon, whole sections of the wall were hacked off as trophies. This fragment ended up in the British museum. This (10)_____ relief of the Goddess Maat with a feather headdress is from a museum in Florence. The only way you can tell that she's the real thing is because she's (11)_____ protective glass. The copies aren't.

7 Comprehension Questions

次の英文がニュースの内容に合っていればT (True)、合っていなければF (False) に丸印を付けよう。また、その根拠とした部分に下線を引いておこう。

Track 42

[T / F] (1)　We can learn many things about the past from the tomb.
[T / F] (2)　It is difficult to understand what is written on the walls.
[T / F] (3)　Technology can be used to understand the tomb.

Track 43

[T / F] (4)　The "Hall of Beauties" is in a room in Switzerland.
[T / F] (5)　Factum Arte made a copy of Seti's tomb.
[T / F] (6)　To make the molds, it is necessary to touch the walls.

Track 44

[T / F] (7)　The Seti replica was made in one piece.
[T / F] (8)　Paintings were done of the tomb when it was discovered.
[T / F] (9)　Pieces of the tomb can be seen around the world.

8 Summary

次の文章はニュースの要約です。空所に適切な語を入れてみよう。

In 1817, the (1.　　　　) of Seti I was discovered by the Great Belzoni, who was amazed by its (2.　　　　) interior. Many years later, Adam Lowe, a man with an (3.　　　　) with this place, made a (4.　　　　) of it. This (5.　　　　) recreation was made by scanning the walls, milling the pieces, (6.　　　　) them, and finally covering the facsimile with a flexible (7.　　　　). Adam Lowe believes that we can learn a lot about people's thinking and (8.　　　　) from these historical places.

● **Try this, too!** ●

ニュースの内容について、以下の質問をクラスメイトと話しあってみよう。

Imagine that 200 years have passed. What kind of things that we have in 2019 will still exist? Discuss with your partner or in your group.

Unit 5 Pigments

不思議な顔料

絵具に色を与える顔料。ハーバード大学美術館には多くの顔料が保存されています。どのような特徴があるのか、見てみましょう。

1 Warm Up

(1) What is your favorite color?

(2) How many colors do you know?

(3) Do some colors make you feel sad, happy, or some other emotion?

2 Vocabulary

この課のニュースに出てくる重要単語の意味を選んでみよう。発音も確認してみよう。

1. pigment (　)
2. cactus (　)
3. deteriorate (　)
4. substance (　)
5. liquid (　)
6. mummy (　)
7. toxic (　)
8. restoration (　)

a. 有毒（な）　e. サボテン
b. 液体　　　　f. 復元
c. ミイラ　　　g. 悪化する
d. 顔料　　　　h. 物質

Notes この課のニュースに出てくるやや難解な語（句）です。予め参考確認しておこう。

The Harvard Art Museums: ハーバード大学美術館／**beetle:** 甲虫／**come off:** ～落ちる／**dried urine:** 乾燥した尿／**chunk:** かたまり／**lead:** 鉛／**particle:** 粒子／**binding medium:** 結合溶剤／**decade:** 10年／**rattan palm:** 藤ヤシ／**source:** 源／**handle:** 扱う／**resin:** 松やに／**arsenic scent:** ヒ素／**left out:** 取り残された

3 Vocabulary Exercise

2 で確認した Vocabulary を使って、必要があれば変化形にした上で空欄を埋めてみよう。

(1) Unfortunately, my grandmother's health has _____ recently.

(2) After the temple's _____, it looked much better than before.

(3) John knew to be careful picking mushrooms because some are _____.

(4) In the summer, you should drink plenty of _____, like water or tea.

(5) Inside the tomb, there were _____ of Egyptian kings and queens.

(6) Artists use different _____ to create the paint colors they want.

(7) _____ are some of the only plants that can live in a dry desert.

(8) A spider produces a silky _____ from its body to make a web.

4 Topic Paragraph

ニュースの出だしの部分を確認し、下の［正誤］問題に答えてみよう。

AZUZ: Next, a great big story about pigments: substances that become paint or ink when they're mixed with liquid. The Harvard Art Museums have more than 2500 pigment samples. Their collection started over a hundred years ago when a museum director noticed that the medieval paintings he brought home were quickly deteriorating. So, he started collecting pigments as well as paintings.

True / False Questions

(1) Pigments are a kind of paint.　　　　　　　　　　　　　　　［ True / False ］

(2) The Harvard Art Museums' collection is more than a hundred years old.
　　　　　　　　　　　　　　　　　　　　　　　　　　　　　［ True / False ］

(3) The medieval paintings did not stay in a good condition.　　　［ True / False ］

• • • • • • • • • • • • • • • • • • • **Try this!** •

1 リピーティング！　　　2 オーバーラッピング！　　　3 シャドーイング！

5 Memo

ノートなどに聞こえた単語やフレーズを書きながらニュースを聞いてみよう。

6 Transcript Completion

映像の音声や、ゆっくりと読み直した音声を聴いて空所に適切な語を入れてみよう。

AZUZ: Next, a great big story about pigments: substances that become paint or ink when they're mixed with liquid. The Harvard Art Museums have more than 2500 pigment samples. Their collection started over a hundred years ago when a museum director noticed that the medieval paintings he brought home were quickly deteriorating. So, he started collecting pigments as well as paintings.

NARAYAN KHANDEKAR, DIRECTOR, STRAUS CENTER, HARVARD ART MUSEUM: It can be beetles that come off a cactus. It can be the dried urine of a cow, little insects that grow on an oak tree, a chunk of lead that's soaked in vinegar. It's truly (1)_____.

KHANDEKAR: We're in Harvard University outside the Forbes pigment collection. Pigment is a very small particle of colored material that is mixed in with a binding medium. The pigment gives paint its (2)_____. The Forbes pigment collection has been brought together over several decades. We have around 2,500 pigments. We have a lot of very (3)_____ and very (4)_____ colors. So, this is, I think, one of the more unusually named pigments. It's called Dragon's Blood. It doesn't come from dragons. It comes from rattan palms and it gives a very bright red pigment.

The unusual aspect of Mummy has to do with its source rather than the color itself, and that comes from Egyptian mummies. And it's the resin that's applied to the outside of the bandages. I think the rarest color that we have is actually an entire ball of Indian Yellow, and this is a pigment that is made from the dried urine of cows that are fed only on mango leaves. If you're looking at a work of (5)_____, and you want to understand what is original and what's a restoration, you will take a tiny sample of pigment and (6)_____ it.

A lot of the pigments are actually toxic. You don't want to handle the pigments and then go out to (7)_____. There's a green called Emerald Green that has an arsenic scent to it. We can use them for telling if something is real or not. People will say this is by a certain artist, and we can look at the materials that he used and (8)_____ if those materials were available during that artist's lifetime. If not, then we have to look at who might have painted that

(9)_____. I can't pick a personal favorite. It's like asking to pick a favorite child. No, the other (10)_____ would feel left out.

7 Comprehension Questions

次の英文がニュースの内容に合っていればT (True)、合っていなければF (False) に丸印を付けよう。また、その根拠とした部分に下線を引いておこう。

Track 54

[T / F] (1) Pigments are always living things.
[T / F] (2) Paint has color because of the pigment in it.
[T / F] (3) Dragon's Blood is made of blood.

Track 55

[T / F] (4) Mummy is a pigment made of bandages.
[T / F] (5) Cows are fed with mango leaves to make Indian Yellow.
[T / F] (6) Pigments help us to better understand paintings.

Track 56

[T / F] (7) Some pigments can be dangerous.
[T / F] (8) By looking at pigments we can check if a piece of art was made by a certain artist.
[T / F] (9) Narayan Khandekar does not tell us his favorite pigment.

8 Summary

次の文章はニュースの要約です。空所に適切な語を入れてみよう。

When (1.   ) are mixed with (2.   ), they become paint or ink. There are many different sources of these (3.   ) — beetles that live on (4.   ), cow urine and even the bandages of (5.   ). It is not surprising, therefore, that some of them are (6.   )! The collection in the Harvard Art Museums began because old paintings were (7.   ). These materials can also be used to check if part of a painting is a (8.   ).

•••••••••••••••••••••• **Try this, too!** ••••••••••••••••••••••

ニュースの内容について、以下の質問をクラスメイトと話しあってみよう。

If you have a chance to exhibit pigments in a museum, what would you do? What kinds of displays would you have? Make a plan and do a presentation based on it.

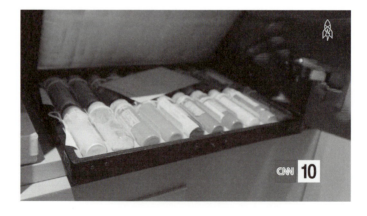

Unit 6 Shopping Tech

未来型ショッピング

現在、いくつかの店舗では無人の精算機が導入されています。将来、こうした技術はどこまで進化するのでしょうか？もはや店員はいらないのでしょうか？

1 Warm Up

(1) Have you ever done your shopping online?

(2) Do you need some advice from a shop assistant when you buy clothes?

(3) Which do you prefer, shopping online or in a store? Why?

2 Vocabulary

この課のニュースに出てくる重要単語の意味を選んでみよう。発音も確認してみよう。

1. replace (　)
2. retail (　)
3. simulation (　)
4. interpersonal (　)
5. outfit (　)
6. realistic (　)
7. partly (　)
8. algorithm (　)

a. 実際の
b. 疑似体験
c. 服
d. 取り換える
e. 人間同士の
f. 小売
g. 演算法
h. 部分的には

Notes この課のニュースに出てくるやや難解な語（句）です。予め参考確認しておこう。

one strike against that: それに対する１つの欠点／**augmented reality:** 拡張現実（現実世界に視覚情報を重複表示させる技術）／**involve:** 関わる／**Echo Look:** 米国アマゾン社の製品で自分の服装を撮影してファッションアドバイスを得られるもの／**Alexa:** 米国アマゾン社が開発した音声操作を可能にするAIアシスタント／**hit or miss:** 運任せの／**take into account:** 考慮に入れる／**nuance:** 微妙な差異

3 Vocabulary Exercise

2 で確認した Vocabulary を使って、必要があれば変化形にした上で空欄を埋めてみよう。

(1) The weather was _____ cloudy, so it wasn't very hot.
(2) Many people say _____ stores will be replaced by online shopping.
(3) Computer programmers use _____ to solve problems.
(4) The CG _____ of a roller coaster was very realistic.
(5) We _____ the old light bulbs with new LED lights.
(6) _____ relationships with other people are important.
(7) My normal summer _____ is simple: shorts and a T-shirt.
(8) His paintings of people are very _____, and look like photos.

4 Topic Paragraph

ニュースの出だしの部分を確認し、下の［正誤］問題に答えてみよう。

AZUZ: From sea to store. Next story brings together business, fashion and technology. We've reported a lot this year on how many U.S. retail companies are closing stores or going out of business, and how that's partly because more Americans are doing their shopping online. But one strike against that is that it doesn't usually allow you to try on clothes before you buy them, to see how they'd actually look on you. Well, some companies are turning to A.R., augmented reality, and V.R., virtual reality, to bring you a step closer to that. What people see are increasingly realistic simulations of actually trying something on.

True / False Questions

(1) Online shopping is causing stores to close. [True / False]
(2) If we shop online, we can never try on the clothes before we buy. [True / False]
(3) Companies are using V.R. to simulate trying on clothes. [True / False]

•••••••••••••••••• **Try this!** ••••••••••••••••••
1 リピーティング！   2 オーバーラッピング！   3 シャドーイング！

5 Memo

ノートなどに聞こえた単語やフレーズを書きながらニュースを聞いてみよう。

6 Transcript Completion

映像の音声や、ゆっくりと読み直した音声を聴いて空所に適切な語を入れてみよう。

AZUZ: From sea to store. Next story brings together business, fashion and technology. We've reported a lot this year on how many U.S. retail companies are closing stores or going out of business, and how that's partly because more Americans are doing their shopping online. But one strike against that is that it doesn't usually allow you to try on clothes before you buy them, to see how they'd actually look on you. Well, some companies are turning to A.R., augmented reality, and V.R., virtual reality, to bring you a step closer to that. What people see are increasingly realistic simulations of actually trying something on.

RACHEL CRANE, CNN CORRESPONDENT (voice-over): In the future, getting dressed may involve a lot more tech than you ever (1)_____.

NEHA SINGH, FOUNDER & CEO, OBSESS: So, this is where, you know, you can see, like, it's really photorealistic (2)_____, even though it's 3D.

CRANE (on camera): I see the fur, like, moving.

CRANE (voice-over): First up, Amazon's Echo Look. They call it a style assistant. So, we put it to the test...

(on camera): Alexa, (3)_____ a (4)_____.

(voice-over): ...against an actual stylist.

UNIDENTIFIED MALE: I want to see. Oh my gosh, that's crazy.

CRANE (on camera): And there we go. Let's do a style (5)_____.

(voice-over): Its review takes some time, but when it's done, it ranks which one it likes the best.

(on camera): According to Alexa, I am supposed to wear the (6)_____ (7)_____ daytime outfit. Oh, they say the colors better for you. The outfit shape works better for you.

(voice-over): Amazon's algorithm doesn't stop at telling you what looks good. It also tries to sell you clothes. But its suggestions are hit or miss.

And while the Echo Look may help you (8)_____ between two looks, it can't take into account the nuance of where you're going.

(on camera): When you hear about the (9)_____ of all these advanced technologies, do you worry about the future of your job?

UNIDENTIFIED MALE: For me, I personally don't. I think with, you know, the future of technology and fashion I think will (10)_____, like, production and retail. As a stylist, there's just that, you know, interpersonal communication that you can't (11)_____.

7 Comprehension Questions

次の英文がニュースの内容に合っていればT (True)、合っていなければF (False) に丸印を付けよう。また、その根拠とした部分に下線を引いておこう。

Track 66

[T / F] (1) The use of technology in the future could be greater than we thought.
[T / F] (2) The 3D simulation images don't look real.
[T / F] (3) They are comparing style technology and a professional stylist.

Track 67

[T / F] (4) The stylist is surprised by the results of using technology.
[T / F] (5) Alexa makes suggestions about what Rachel Crane should wear.
[T / F] (6) The Amazon app doesn't make any mistakes.

Track 68

[T / F] (7) Echo Look is affected by the user's destination.
[T / F] (8) The stylist believes clothes production will benefit from technology.
[T / F] (9) People communicating with each other are not important when choosing clothes.

8 Summary

次の文章はニュースの要約です。空所に適切な語を入れてみよう。

Recently, more and more (1.   ) clothing stores have been (2.   ) by online shopping. The problem with this is that shoppers can't try on a new (3.   ) or get any feedback through (4.   ) communication with a shop assistant or stylist. Online retailers are using virtual and augmented reality to create (5.   ), and a variety of applications to (6.   ) make up for this. Using a headset, shoppers can see (7.   ) 3D images of the items they want to buy. Using (8.   ), applications try to help shoppers choose clothes that suit them.

• Try this, too! •

ニュースの内容について、以下の質問をクラスメイトと話しあってみよう。

Discuss the advantages and disadvantages of A.R. or V.R. in shopping. Will it be popular in Japan?

Vocabulary / Idioms in the News
From Units 4-6

ここでは上記 Unit に出てきた表現を特集して学習できます。

Exercise

左側の英単語・語句の意味を、右側の日本語訳と正しくつなげてみよう。

1.	end up in ( )	a.	店じまいする
2.	at any point ( )	b.	〜に一歩近づく
3.	build a dialogue ( )	c.	〜にいきつく
4.	work of art ( )	d.	運任せの
5.	bring together ( )	e.	どの点においても
6.	(feel) left out ( )	f.	芸術作品
7.	go out of business ( )	g.	取り残された（と感じる）
8.	one strike against (something) ( )	h.	対話を構築する
9.	one step closer to ( )	i.	まとめる
10.	hit or miss ( )	j.	（何か）に対する一つの欠点

Unit 7 Origami

科学者で折り紙職人

日本では子どものときに一度は遊ぶ折り紙。この折り紙にデザインやエンジニアの観点から取り組んでいるアメリカの物理学者の話を聞いてみましょう。

1 Warm Up

(1) What is origami? What can you make using origami?

(2) Can you think of any uses of origami in science?

(3) What was your hobby in your childhood? Is it still your hobby?

2 Vocabulary

この課のニュースに出てくる重要単語の意味を選んでみよう。発音も確認してみよう。

1. mathematician ( )
2. attribute (n) ( )
3. physicist ( )
4. pursue ( )
5. quit ( )
6. achieve ( )
7. equation ( )
8. fold ( )

a. 数学者　　e. 続ける
b. 物理学者　f. やめる
c. 達成する　g. 特性
d. 折る　　　h. 方程式

Notes この課のニュースに出てくるやや難解な語（句）です。予め参考確認しておこう。

complicated: 複雑な／exoskeleton: 外骨格／predetermined: あらかじめ決められた／unfold: 開く／unexpected: 予想できない／entire life: 生涯／cylindrical: 円筒／inflate: 膨らむ／bundle: 束／relatively: 比較的／driving force: 原動力

3 Vocabulary Exercise

2 で確認した Vocabulary を使って、必要があれば変化形にした上で空欄を埋めてみよう。

(1) If you work very hard, it is possible to _____ great success.
(2) JAXA hired _____ to design rockets for the space program.
(3) To do origami well, it is necessary to _____ the paper perfectly.
(4) Tom is _____ a successful career in New York as an actor.
(5) She _____ her job after only a month because it was too difficult.
(6) My uncle is good with numbers, so he became a _____.
(7) On the math test, I had to solve many difficult _____.
(8) My teacher's best _____ is that she is always positive.

4 Topic Paragraph

ニュースの出だしの部分を確認し、下の［正誤］問題に答えてみよう。

AZUZ: Origami, which comes from the Japanese words "fold" and "paper", is increasingly being used to solve complicated engineering problems. On a "10 Out of 10" segment last month, we covered an MIT project on origami robots. They included a small machine and a plastic exoskeleton that folded into a predetermined shape when it's heated. Well, a former NASA physicist has folded his love for origami into his career as a mathematician.

True / False Questions

(1) Paper folding can be used in engineering.　　　　［ True / False ］
(2) CNN 10 has never had a report about origami before.　　［ True / False ］
(3) A former NASA scientist is using origami in his work.　　［ True / False ］

・・・・・・・・・・・・・・・・・・・ Try this! ・・・・・・・・・・・・・・・・・・・

1　リピーティング！　　2　オーバーラッピング！　　3　シャドーイング！

5 Memo

ノートなどに聞こえた単語やフレーズを書きながらニュースを聞いてみよう。

6 Transcript Completion

映像の音声や、ゆっくりと読み直した音声を聴いて空所に適切な語を入れてみよう。

AZUZ: Origami, which comes from the Japanese words "fold" and "paper," is increasingly being used to solve complicated engineering problems. On a "10 Out of 10" segment last month, we covered an MIT project on origami robots. They included a small machine and a plastic exoskeleton that folded into a predetermined shape when it's heated. Well, a former NASA physicist has folded his love for origami into his career as a mathematician.

ROBERT LANG, PHYSICIST & ORIGAMI ARTIST: One of the most important attributes of origami is once we have studied and understood the way paper folds and unfolds, we can apply those patterns to things that are very different from paper. I hope by bringing the tools of mathematics into my origami design, that I can then fold something that's beautiful and that's unexpected. My name is Robert Lang and I'm a physicist and an origami artist.

LANG: Origami is the Japanese name for the art of folded paper, and most origami is folded from a single sheet of paper with no cuts or (1)_____. I have loved origami my entire life. I pursued it ever since I was a kid, but my study was science and engineering. I worked for NASA, doing research on lasers. But throughout that whole time, I had been pursuing origami, developing (2)_____ and writing books.

So in 2001, I quit my job to try to make a career out of origami. I've worked on a couple of different folding patterns that were round and would wrap into a cylindrical geometry to fit into a (3)_____. And I developed an airbag in a car that inflates from a small folded bundle. So, whenever an engineer creates something that opens and closes in a controlled way, they can make use of the folding patterns of origami. Over the years, math has (4)_____ me to realize as an artist, shapes and creations that I couldn't achieve any other way. Traditional origami was relatively simple. The designs would have taken maybe (5)_____ or (6)_____ steps at most. But today, origami pieces can be so complicated that they can have tens, hundreds, maybe even a (7)_____ steps.

When I'm folding, it's like working with an old friend. It's like (8)_____ with a partner whose moves I know. If I move this way, I know my partner's going to move that way and so, I explore the math, develop the equations, solve the equations, create the folding pattern, and then I find out what it looks like. And as often as not, it is (9)_____. For me, the driving force is that there's always something new to try, a new problem, a new subject, a new shape that I didn't think I was able to create before but now I think I know how to realize it. And each time I (10)_____ a problem, you get this wonderful feeling and you want more of those feelings.

7 Comprehension Questions

次の英文がニュースの内容に合っていればT (True)、合っていなければF (False) に丸印を付けよう。また、その根拠とした部分に下線を引いておこう。

Track 78

[T / F]　(1)　Robert Lang thinks we can apply the patterns found in origami to other things.

[T / F]　(2)　By using mathematics, the scientist hopes to make better origami.

[T / F]　(3)　Robert Lang was a physicist and after than an origami artist.

Track 79

[T / F]　(4)　Now, this origami artist makes things that go in vehicles.

[T / F]　(5)　Origami can be useful to people when they open things.

[T / F]　(6)　Mathematics means that Robert Lang can make simpler origami.

Track 80

[T / F]　(7)　The scientist says that he likes dancing.

[T / F]　(8)　Using mathematics, a beautiful thing is always created.

[T / F]　(9)　When Robert Lang makes a new shape, he feels good.

8 Summary

次の文章はニュースの要約です。空所に適切な語を入れてみよう。

Robert Lang is a (1.   ) and a (2.   ) who loves origami, the art of (3.   ) paper. He has (4.   ) the study of origami for a long time, even writing books on the topic, until he (5.   ) his job in 2001 in order to make origami his career. Robert Lang makes use of origami's main (6.   ), an understanding of the way things fold and unfold, to help in the design of airbags and rockets. He is able to (7.   ) new origami shapes by using math to make and solve (8.   ).

•••••••••••••••••••••• **Try this, too!** ••••••••••••••••••••••

ニュースの内容について、以下の質問をクラスメイトと話しあってみよう。

Do some online research about interesting origami shapes and tell your classmates about them.

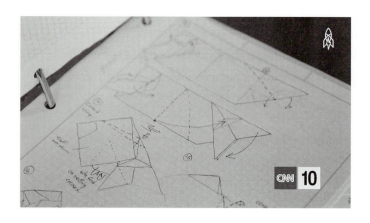

Unit 8 Ice Cream

アイスクリーム大学

デザートとして人気の高いアイスクリーム。アメリカの大学ではアイスクリームに特化した授業があるようです。その担当教授の話を聞いてみましょう。

1 Warm Up

(1) Do you know how to make ice cream?

(2) What is your favorite flavor of ice cream?

(3) What kind of things can we learn from a lecture about ice cream?

2 Vocabulary

この課のニュースに出てくる重要単語の意味を選んでみよう。発音も確認してみよう。

1. forefront (　　)　5. ingredient (　　)
2. annual (　　)　6. purist (　　)
3. authority (　　)　7. herd (　　)
4. frozen (　　)　8. appetizing (　　)

a. 年に一度の　e. 材料
b. 最前線　f. 群れ
c. 食欲をそそる　g. 冷凍（の）
d. 権威　h. 純粋主義者

Notes この課のニュースに出てくるやや難解な語（句）です。予め参考確認しておこう。

101: 大学の基礎的な入門講義／**Penn State University:** ペンシルバニア州立大学／**processing:** 加工／**turn out:** わかる／**pretty** (adv.): かなり／**Unilever, Nestle, Breyers, Ben and Jerry's:** いずれもアイスクリーム関連の食品会社／**creamery:** 乳製品製造所／**naturally occuring:** 天然に生まれる／**figure out:** 解明する／**Holstein:** ホルスタイン牛／**dulce de leche:**（ドゥルセ・デ・レチェ）固体または液体のキャラメル。伝統的なラテンアメリカの糖菓

3 Vocabulary Exercise

2 で確認したVocabularyを使って、必要があれば変化形にした上で空欄を埋めてみよう。

(1) The secret _____ to the ramen soup is chopped garlic.

(2) The fruit looked so _____ that he became very hungry.

(3) Professor Ortiz is an _____ on computers, so he knows a lot.

(4) _____ fees must be paid every year in December.

(5) The researchers were at the _____ of a new science.

(6) Sometimes I buy _____ vegetables rather than fresh vegetables.

(7) In the field, a large _____ of cows chewed grass.

(8) Anna is a _____ about tea, and likes it made in a traditional way.

4 Topic Paragraph

ニュースの出だしの部分を確認し、下の［正誤］問題に答えてみよう。

AZUZ: Up next, Ice Cream 101: Introduction to Frozen Desserts. This is a real course at Penn State University, one in which I'd probably get a D, for delicious! The annual two-day class covers everything from the formula, to the processing of ice cream and it's one appetizing great big story.

True / False Questions

(1) We can study about frozen desserts at Penn State University.　　［True / False］

(2) Azuz doesn't think that he would like the course.　　［True / False］

(3) The course is held every two years.　　［True / False］

• **Try this!** •

1 リピーティング！　　**2** オーバーラッピング！　　**3** シャドーイング！

5 Memo

ノートなどに聞こえた単語やフレーズを書きながらニュースを聞いてみよう。

6 Transcript Completion

映像の音声や、ゆっくりと読み直した音声を聴いて空所に適切な語を入れてみよう。

AZUZ: Up next, Ice Cream 101: Introduction to Frozen Desserts. This is a real course at Penn State University, one in which I'd probably get a D, for delicious! The annual two-day class covers everything from the formula to the processing of ice cream, and it's one appetizing great big story.

REPORTER: Americans, we love ice cream. Each person eats about (1)_____ quarts of it per year, and that's for one big reason: it tastes amazing. But someone had to teach Ben and Jerry's how to do it. Turns out, that guy, he works at Penn State.

REPORTER: This is Dr. Bob Robert... hold on. Okay, this is Dr. Bob Roberts. He teaches ice cream courses at Penn State.

DR. BOB ROBERTS, HEAD OF FOOD SCIENCE, PENN STATE: I do. I have two courses: Ice Cream Short Course, and Ice Cream 101.

REPORTER: Side note: these are the type of books ice cream (2)_____ read. Okay, back to the story.

ROBERTS: Part of the reason that ice cream is so good in the U.S. is that we've been teaching ice cream for (3)_____ years.

REPORTER: And Bob, he's been teaching at Penn State for (4)_____ of those and he's had some pretty famous students.

ROBERTS: (5)_____ like Unilever, Nestle, Breyers, Ben and Jerry's — you name the company, they've sent people here.

REPORTER: That's because the Penn State creamery is on the forefront of ice cream technology.

ROBERTS: Ice cream is a formulated food. There is no naturally occurring ice cream. You have to put the ingredients together and (6)_____ it to make ice cream.

REPORTER: Bob and his department, they spend their time figuring out how to make ice cream even better.

ROBERTS: When we look at studying ice cream, we study ice cream from cow to the cone. So, we look at what happens on the (7)_____, what happens with the milk.

REPORTER: Wait, there's a farm?

ROBERTS: We have a herd of about (8)_____ or so milking Holsteins and, yes, they are on campus.

REPORTER: So, yeah, he knows ice cream, but he says that he's not an ice cream purist.

ROBERTS: I'm not sure what an ice cream purist is, but I wouldn't eat frozen (9)_____ if I had the opportunity to eat ice cream.

REPORTER: Yeah, well, that does make sense considering he is the authority on ice cream. Bob, what's your favorite (10)_____?

ROBERTS: Hmm, dulce de leche.

REPORTER: Um, yeah.

7 Comprehension Questions

次の英文がニュースの内容に合っていればT (True)、合っていなければF (False) に丸印を付けよう。また、その根拠とした部分に下線を引いておこう。

Track 90

[T / F] (1) A lot of ice cream is eaten in the U.S. every year.

[T / F] (2) Ben and Jerry's taught Dr. Bob Roberts how to make ice cream.

[T / F] (3) Ice Cream 101 is a course taught at Penn State.

Track 91

[T / F] (4) How to make ice cream has been taught in the U.S. for 25 years.

[T / F] (5) Famous ice cream companies send their employees to Penn State.

[T / F] (6) Ice cream is made by processing ingredients.

Track 92

[T / F] (7) Dr. Bob Roberts studies the whole process of making ice cream.

[T / F] (8) There is a farm on the campus of Penn State.

[T / F] (9) Dr. Bob Roberts prefers frozen yogurt to ice cream.

8 Summary

次の文章はニュースの要約です。空所に適切な語を入れてみよう。

Dr. Bob Roberts is an (1.   ) on making ice-cream, and though he does prefer ice cream to (2.   ) yogurt, he denies he is an ice-cream (3.   ). He teaches an (4.   ) "Ice Cream 101" course at Penn State University, where many famous ice cream makers have learned how to process the (5.   ) in order to make (6.   ) ice cream. This school has its own (7.   ) of cows and when it comes to ice cream technology, it is on the (8.   ).

•••••••••••••••••••••• **Try this, too!** ••••••••••••••••••••••

ニュースの内容について、以下の質問をクラスメイトと話しあってみよう。

Imagine that you have a chance to create your own university course related to your interest. Describe the details (for example, a syllabus) of your course.

Unit 9 Nigerian Women's Bobsled Team

ナイジェリア出身の女性ボブスレー選手

ウインタースポーツのひとつであるボブスレー。この競技にナイジェリアの選手が参加することになりました。その意気込みを聞いてみましょう。

1 Warm Up

(1) What is bobsledding?

(2) Would you like to try bobsledding? Why or why not?

(3) What do you know about Nigeria? What kind of images do you have?

2 Vocabulary

この課のニュースに出てくる重要単語の意味を選んでみよう。発音も確認してみよう。

Disc 2 / 1

1. represent ( )
2. qualify ( )
3. handicap ( )
4. resilience ( )
5. compete in ( )
6. ecstatic ( )
7. segue ( )
8. transition ( )

a. マイナスにする
b. 逆境力
c. 代表する
d. 資格要件を満たす
e. 移行
f. すみやかに移る
g. 非常に喜んでいる
h. 参加する

Notes この課のニュースに出てくるやや難解な語（句）です。予め参考確認しておこう。

set to: 〜することになっている／**gracefully:** 快く／**the fear of the unknown:** 未知への恐怖／**thrive:** 成功する／**take in:** 取り入れる／**by all accounts:** 誰から聞いても／**take chances:** 思い切って何かをする／**hammer:** 作り上げる／**makeshift:** 間に合わせの／**scraps:** がらくた／**the Mayflower:** メイフラワー号（選手達がガレージで制作した木製のそりの名前）／**catapult:** 一気に伸ばす／**all of a sudden:** 突然

3 Vocabulary Exercise

2 で確認した Vocabulary を使って、必要があれば変化形にした上で空欄を埋めてみよう。

(1) The rescue has been _____ by heavy rain and strong wind.
(2) The _____ from childhood to adulthood takes many years.
(3) During the sunset the sky _____ from light to dark.
(4) To _____ for the Olympics, you must be very good at your sport.
(5) The children were so _____ at the good news that they cheered loudly.
(6) The manager will _____ the company at the convention.
(7) The two rival teams will _____ the championship game.
(8) John's _____ showed everyone that he did not give up easily.

4 Topic Paragraph

ニュースの出だしの部分を確認し、下の[正誤]問題に答えてみよう。

AZUZ: Moving west from Saudi Arabia to the African country of Nigeria. It's had a number of success stories in the Olympic Games, like when its soccer team won gold in 1996. But Nigeria has never won a medal — or even competed — in the Winter Olympics. Next February, three athletes representing Nigeria are set to compete in bobsledding. This is the first bobsled team for any African country. The women have already qualified and say they're ecstatic. Their driver, Seun Adigun, was born in the U.S. to Nigerian parents. She represented Nigeria in the 2012 Summer Games and she spoke to CNN about the transition from one type of track to another.

True / False Questions

(1) Nigeria has never won a medal in the Olympics.　　　　　　　　[True / False]
(2) The bobsled team from Nigeria is the first one from Africa.　　　[True / False]
(3) Seun Adigun has never participated in the Olympics before.　　　[True / False]

••••••••••••••••••••••••• **Try this!** •••••••••••••••••••••••••
1 リピーティング！　　**2** オーバーラッピング！　　**3** シャドーイング！

5 Memo

ノートなどに聞こえた単語やフレーズを書きながらニュースを聞いてみよう。

6 Transcript Completion

映像の音声や、ゆっくりと読み直した音声を聴いて空所に適切な語を入れてみよう。

AZUZ: Moving west from Saudi Arabia to the African country of Nigeria. It's had a number of success stories in the Olympic Games, like when its soccer team won gold in 1996. But Nigeria has never won a medal — or even competed — in the Winter Olympics. Next February, three athletes representing Nigeria are set to compete in bobsledding. This is the first bobsled team for any African country. The women have already qualified and say they're ecstatic. Their driver, Seun Adigun, was born in the U.S. to Nigerian parents. She represented Nigeria in the 2012 Summer Games and she spoke to CNN about the transition from one type of track to another.

SEUN ADIGUN, NIGERIAN WOMEN'S BOBSLED DRIVER: This is beyond a dream come true, you know, to be able to bring something back to not only the country of Nigeria, which has so gracefully given me my family, you know, my (1)_____ and everything that I stand by, but also, to the continent of Africa and the world. You know, just kind of bring a gift for people to know that resilience is something that you can actually live to (2)_____ and that the fear of the unknown doesn't need to be something that limits your ability to thrive in life. I mean, I think that those qualities in itself will really, really be important for everyone to be able to take in.

RIHANNON JONES, CNN WORLD SPORT: Now, you mentioned there the fear of the unknown. Let's stay with that word "fear." It's a pretty (3)_____ (4)_____ by all accounts, is it not?

ADIGUN: Fear is really just another (5)_____ to learn. Fear is…, it shouldn't be something that handicaps your idea of what it means to be successful. It should be a driving force to how you live and take chances and do things that you may not have even thought were (6)_____.

JONES: And I understand, it all began in a Texas garage just a few years ago, where you hammered together a makeshift sled out of wood and scraps. I mean, it's quite (7)_____ what you've achieved from what you... you were making in that garage. Talk us through it.

ADIGUN: Yes, the Mayflower, you know, really helped to catapult my ability to learn how to bobsled, as well as to help teach it. And, I mean, look at it now, that was a learning (8)_____ before and now, all of a sudden, I'm segued into being in real bobsleds. I mean, look at just the transition from wooden sled to real sleds. I mean, this is absolutely (9)_____.

7 Comprehension Questions

次の英文がニュースの内容に合っていればT (True)、合っていなければF (False) に丸印を付けよう。また、その根拠とした部分に下線を引いておこう。

Track 5

[T / F] (1) Adigun wants to give something back to Nigeria.
[T / F] (2) Adigun thinks that she can show others resilience.
[T / F] (3) Adigun thinks fear always stops us from being successful.

Track 6

[T / F] (4) Bobsledding is thought to be a scary sport.
[T / F] (5) Adigun thinks of fear in a negative way.
[T / F] (6) We can use fear to do amazing things.

Track 7

[T / F] (7) Adigun's first sled was expensive.
[T / F] (8) Adigun's first sled was made in a garage.
[T / F] (9) Adigun is amazed by the transition she has experienced.

8 Summary

次の文章はニュースの要約です。空所に適切な語を入れてみよう。

Seun Adigun is the driver in the Nigerian bobsledding team, which has (1.   ) for the Winter Olympics. This is the first time an African country will be (2.   ) at the games and the athletes are (3.   ). Adigun (4.   ) the Summer Olympics in 2012 before her (5.   ) to bobsledding. She built and practiced with a wooden bobsled before she (6.   ) to a real one. She believes that she has learnt (7.   ) through her experience and that fear should not (8.   ) anybody.

• Try this, too! •

ニュースの内容について、以下の質問をクラスメイトと話しあってみよう。

What can athletes do to help people in their countries? Discuss with your classmates and present your ideas.

Vocabulary / Idioms in the News
From Units 7-9

ここでは上記Unitに出てきた表現を特集して学習できます。

Exercise

左側の英単語・語句の意味を、右側の日本語訳と正しくつなげてみよう。

1.	make a career out of	( )	a.	誰から聞いても
2.	driving force	( )	b.	時間を費やす
3.	as often as not	( )	c.	（何か）を一部始終話す
4.	on the forefront	( )	d.	突然
5.	spend time	( )	e.	思い切って何かをする
6.	figure out	( )	f.	大抵
7.	take chances	( )	g.	〜を生涯の仕事にする
8.	talk through (something)	( )	h.	最前線に
9.	all of a sudden	( )	i.	原動力
10.	by all accounts	( )	j.	解明する

Unit 10 Zoo Dog

動物を管轄する動物

アメリカの動物園には動物を飼育する動物（犬）がいます。その犬の生い立ちと仕事ぶりを見てみましょう。

1 Warm Up

(1) How often do you go to zoos?

(2) What is your favorite animal in the zoo?

(3) What are some things that dogs can do?

2 Vocabulary

この課のニュースに出てくる重要単語の意味を選んでみよう。発音も確認してみよう。

1. aggresion (　)　5. interact (　)
2. upset (　)　6. on alert (　)
3. appropriate (　)　7. cue (　)
4. nanny (　)　8. nursery (　)

a. 合図　e. 飼育室
b. 子守　f. 適切な
c. 敵対心　g. 注意深く見守って
d. 怒る　h. 交わる

Notes この課のニュースに出てくるやや難解な語（句）です。予め参考確認しておこう。

every dog has his (its) day: どの犬にでも最高の時がある／**Georgia Bulldogs:** 米国州立ジョージア大学のスポーツチームの呼称／**a far cry from:** 〜とは全く違って／**snap:** 切れる／**kind of like:** どことなく／**Botanical Garden:** 植物園／**a rescue (rescue center):** 救護施設／**companion dog:** 付き添い犬／**take a nap:** 昼寝をする／**cheetah:** チーター／**ocelot:** オセロット（中・南米産のヒョウに似た大きなヤマネコ）／**takin:** ターキン（ヒマラヤ東部産の大型重量のヤギ）／**warthog:** イボイノシシ／**wallaby:** ワラビー／**cub:** （肉食獣の）子供／**second set of eyes:** 第二番目の目／**grunt:** 低くうなる

3 Vocabulary Exercise

2 で確認した Vocabulary を使って、必要があれば変化形にした上で空欄を埋めてみよう。

(1) Babies are sometimes raised in a _____ by caregivers.
(2) The teacher pointed and nodded to Reiko, a _____ for her to start.
(3) He was _____ because the game was cancelled due to bad weather.
(4) At the party, the boys and girls _____ with each other a lot.
(5) The firemen are _____ 24 hours a day in case of a fire.
(6) While at the office, you should wear the _____ uniform.
(7) The _____ took care of the children while the parents were at work.
(8) He showed signs of _____, so a therapist talked to him.

4 Topic Paragraph

ニュースの出だしの部分を確認し、下の［正誤］問題に答えてみよう。

AZUZ: It's been said every dog has his day. I'm hoping today is that day for my Georgia Bulldogs, but Blakely is the name of a rescued Australian Shepherd who had his own day named after him by the city of Cincinnati, Ohio. Why? Because Blakely, who works at the Cincinnati Zoo, has served and succeeded as a nanny for a number of animals who are a far cry from his own species. It's today's "10 Out of 10" and the "Great Big Story."

True / False Questions

(1) The city of Cincinnati thinks that Blakely has done a good job.   ［ True / False ］
(2) The Australian Shepherd's work is like being a mother.   ［ True / False ］
(3) Blakely helps only other dogs at the zoo.   ［ True / False ］

••••••••••••••••••••••• **Try this!** •••••••••••••••••••••••

1 リピーティング！   2 オーバーラッピング！   3 シャドーイング！

5 Memo

ノートなどに聞こえた単語やフレーズを書きながらニュースを聞いてみよう。

6 Transcript Completion

映像の音声や、ゆっくりと読み直した音声を聴いて空所に適切な語を入れてみよう。

AZUZ: It's been said every dog has his day. I'm hoping today is that day for my Georgia Bulldogs, but Blakely is the name of a rescued Australian Shepherd who had his own day named after him by the city of Cincinnati, Ohio. Why? Because Blakely, who works at the Cincinnati Zoo, has served and succeeded as a nanny for a number of animals who are a far cry from his own species. It's today's "10 Out of 10" and the "Great Big Story."

DAWN STRASSER, HEAD NURSERY KEEPER: Blakely has the most (1)_____ job in Cincinnati Zoo. He has to play with babies all the time. He's never shown any aggression or snapped. If he gets upset, kind of like any mom would, he just leaves the (2)_____.

UNIDENTIFIED FEMALE: You are so cute!

STRASSER: My name is Dawn Strasser and we're at the Cincinnati Zoo and Botanical Gardens. Blakely is a 5-year-old Australian Shepherd. We got him from a rescue, and I use him in a nursery as a nanny or a companion dog.

UNIDENTIFIED FEMALE: This is about you and you're taking a nap.

STRASSER: Blakeley's here for the main (3)_____ of teaching the babies the correct animal cues as they grow up, so when they are introduced back to their own kind, they know what appropriate (4)_____ is. He teaches them how to play, how to interact. I can tell them "No, don't (5)_____ (6)_____," but I'm not an animal and I don't give the same cues that he can. So, we make a great team.

Blakely has worked with cheetahs, ocelots, a takin, feathered foxes, a warthog, wallabies... to name a few. He's working with (7)_____ baby cheetahs right now. It's been a long seven weeks for him with these little cheetah cubs and he's, I think, (8)_____ as he's on alert for 24 hours a day. If they start making too much noise, he'll come and get us, like, something's not right, something's not right. He's kind of like a second set of eyes for us too. A lot of times, they still (9)_____ each other, like Dale, the takin he raised. When they see each other, Dale'll still run up in front and grunt at him and he'll kind of jump up on the wall and kind of like, hey, how you doing?

STRASSER: Yeah, well, I like to think I have an (10)_____ but I'm pretty sure it's his.

7 Comprehension Questions

次の英文がニュースの内容に合っていればT (True)、合っていなければF (False) に丸印を付けよう。また、その根拠とした部分に下線を引いておこう。

Track 17

[T / F] (1) Dawn thinks that playing with babies is difficult.
[T / F] (2) Blakely is always happy with his work.
[T / F] (3) The Australian Shepherd was born at the zoo.

Track 18

[T / F] (4) Blakely's main work is to show animals how to interact with people.
[T / F] (5) Some animals don't know how to interact with the same species.
[T / F] (6) Dawn can give more appropriate cues than Blakely.

Track 19

[T / F] (7) The dog has no time to relax, so he is tired.
[T / F] (8) If there is a problem, Blakely can always solve it himself.
[T / F] (9) The animals Blakely has helped often recognize him.

8 Summary

次の文章はニュースの要約です。空所に適切な語を入れてみよう。

Blakely is an Australian Shepherd who works in the (1.   ) of the Cincinnati Zoo as a (2.   ). His job is to (3.   ) with different animals and teach them the correct (4.   ) so that they can learn how to behave in an (5.   ) way. Even though Blakely can be working and (6.   ) all day, he has never shown any (7.   ). He does get (8.   ) sometimes, but when he does, he just leaves the room.

• **Try this, too!** •

ニュースの内容について、以下の質問をクラスメイトと話しあってみよう。

Research dogs with special abilities. What are they? Introduce these in a presentation in English.

Unit 11 Google Before Google

グーグルがなかった時代には

今やネット検索といえばGoogle。でもGoogleがなかった頃はどうしていたのでしょうか？ニューヨーク公立図書館の例を見てみましょう。

1 Warm Up

(1) How often do you use Google?

(2) If you have a question, which do you like better, asking someone or researching it yourself?

(3) If you needed someone to talk to, what would you do?

2 Vocabulary

この課のニュースに出てくる重要単語の意味を選んでみよう。発音も確認してみよう。

1. current   (　)   5. chase   (　)
2. librarian (　)   6. department (　)
3. squirrel   (　)   7. honestly   (　)
4. tame   (　)   8. serrated   (　)

a. 正直に   e. 最近の
b. 追いかける   f. リス
c. 司書   g. ギザギザの
d. 手なずける   h. 部署

Notes この課のニュースに出てくるやや難解な語（句）です。予め参考確認しておこう。

popsicle sticks: アイスキャンディー棒／**clowder:** 猫の群れ／**NYPL:** (New York Public Libraryの頭文字)／**reach out to:** 〜に連絡しようとする／**Acapulco:** アカプルコ（メキシコのリゾート都市）／**Plato:** プラトン（哲学者）／**Aristotle:** アリストテレス（哲学者）／**Socrates:** ソクラテス（哲学者）／**one and the same:** 同一の／**oftentimes:** 多くの場合／**Great White Shark:** ホオジロザメ

3 Vocabulary Exercise

2 で確認した Vocabulary を使って、必要があれば変化形にした上で空欄を埋めてみよう。

(1) The lion was _____ over many years, and now it isn't dangerous.
(2) In order to cut down trees, the saw has a sharp _____ blade.
(3) Taro watched the _____ in the park jump from tree to tree.
(4) In the company's sales _____, Roberto was the top salesperson.
(5) I _____ think it is a good chance to learn from big mistakes.
(6) The cat _____ the mouse, but the mouse was faster and escaped.
(7) The boys were noisy, so the _____ told them to be quiet.
(8) The _____ version of this software will be updated next week.

4 Topic Paragraph

ニュースの出だしの部分を確認し、下の［正誤］問題に答えてみよう。

AZUZ: What was the name of Napoleon's most famous horse? What does it mean when you dream you're being chased by an elephant? Is there a book on how to build with popsicle sticks? Search engines could help you find these answers, but in their current form, they've only been around since the mid-1990s. The New York Public Library has been open since 1911, and if you don't feel like searching through its collection, you can always give 'em a phone call.

True / False Questions

(1) Search engines only help answer important questions.　　［ True / False ］
(2) The New York Public Library has been around longer than search engines.
　　　　　　　　　　　　　　　　　　　　　　　　　　　　　　　　　　　　　　　［ True / False ］
(3) It is possible to contact the New York Public Library by phone.　　［ True / False ］

••••••••••••••••••••••••• **Try this!** •••••••••••••••••••••••••

1　リピーティング！　　2　オーバーラッピング！　　3　シャドーイング！

5 Memo

ノートなどに聞こえた単語やフレーズを書きながらニュースを聞いてみよう。

6 Transcript Completion

映像の音声や、ゆっくりと読み直した音声を聴いて空所に適切な語を入れてみよう。

AZUZ: What was the name of Napoleon's most famous horse? What does it mean when you dream you're being chased by an elephant? Is there a book on how to build with popsicle sticks? Search engines could help you find these answers, but in their current form, they've only been around since the mid-1990s. The New York Public Library has been open since 1911, and if you don't feel like searching through its collection, you can always give 'em a phone call.

UNIDENTIFIED FEMALE: What do you call a group of cats?

UNIDENTIFIED FEMALE: Let me check on that. It's called a clowder of cats.

REPORTER: If you have a question, any question, there's a number you can call.

ROSA CABALLERO-LI, MANAGER, ASK NYPL: Nine, one, seven, two, (1)_____, five, six, nine, seven, (2)_____.

REPORTER: And a librarian at the New York Public Library will try to answer it for you.

UNIDENTIFIED MALE: Hello. Thanks for calling Ask NYPL.

CABALLERO-LI: We have (3)_____ librarians on the team, and we answer any question that you may have over the telephone. In the office today, we have Matthew, Bernard, Sarina, Diane and me. Our department, Ask NYPL, began in (4)_____. We started answering questions over the telephone. But people have been reaching out to librarians for as long as there have been libraries.

REPORTER: The New York Public Library has actually (5)_____ records of some of the more interesting questions they've been asked over the years. Like, is there a full moon every night in Acapulco? Why do 18th century English paintings have so many squirrels in them and how did they tame them so they wouldn't (6)_____ the painter? Are Plato, Aristotle, and Socrates one and the same person? In a world of Google, it's a bit (7)_____ to know that they get around 30,000 calls per year. My question is, why?

CABALLERO-LI: Oftentimes, people might not have access to the technology at home, and I (8)_____ think some just want somebody to talk to.

REPORTER: So, the next time you have a question like, how many teeth does a Great White Shark have, you can call this number.

CABALLERO-LI: Nine, one, seven, (9)_____, seven, five, six, nine, (10)_____, five.

REPORTER: That will ring inside of this building, up on this floor, and maybe Bernard or Rosa will pick up and they'll answer it for you.

CABALLERO-LI: They have about (11)_____ serrated teeth.

7 Comprehension Questions

次の英文がニュースの内容に合っていればT (True)、合っていなければF (False) に丸印を付けよう。また、その根拠とした部分に下線を引いておこう。

Track 29

[T / F] (1) A group of cats is called a clowder of cats.
[T / F] (2) If you call the library, you can ask them questions.
[T / F] (3) Before there were phones, libraries didn't help people.

Track 30

[T / F] (4) All of the questions asked are recorded by the library.
[T / F] (5) One of the questions was about animals in art.
[T / F] (6) Because of Google, the library gets few phone calls.

Track 31

[T / F] (7) People may call the library just to talk to somebody.
[T / F] (8) The phone number for the library is a secret.
[T / F] (9) They cannot answer questions about sharks.

8 Summary

次の文章はニュースの要約です。空所に適切な語を入れてみよう。

In the New York City Library there is a (1._____) you can call if you need the answer to a question. The (2._____) can tell you that a shark has (3._____) teeth or what having an elephant (4._____) you in a dream means. They have been asked why so many (5._____) appear in paintings and how this animal could be (6._____). These questions could be researched using (7._____) search engines like Google but the library still gets a lot of calls, though the staff (8._____) think that some people just call because they are lonely.

• **Try this, too!** •

ニュースの内容について、以下の質問をクラスメイトと話しあってみよう。

What do you think are the good points and bad points of using Google and phoning the library to get the answer to a question? Discuss with your classmates.

Unit 12　3D Food Printing

料理を
3Dプリンターで

新しいテクノロジーとして注目されている3Dプリンター。これを料理に用いたらどんなことが出来るのでしょうか？

1　Warm Up

(1) Are you good at cooking?

(2) What is your favorite dish? Can you explain how to make it?

(3) What is a 3D printer? Have you ever seen or used a 3D printer?

2　Vocabulary

この課のニュースに出てくる重要単語の意味を選んでみよう。発音も確認してみよう。

37

1. dismiss　　　(　)　　5. predict　　　(　)
2. conventional　(　)　　6. resolution　(　)
3. appliance　　(　)　　7. novelty　　　(　)
4. precision　　(　)　　8. dough　　　(　)

a. 生地　　　e. 珍奇な物
b. 精密さ　　f. 予測する
c. 退ける　　g. 分解能
d. 従来の　　h. 電化製品

Notes この課のニュースに出てくるやや難解な語（句）です。予め参考確認しておこう。

machine (v): 機械を使って作る／**figure out:** 見つける／**incorporate:** 組み込む／**as opposed to ~:** 〜とは違って／**accuracy:** 精密さ／**pinpoint:** 極小／**lay it out:** 割り付ける／**goo:** ねばつくもの／**misconception:** 誤解／**appetizing:** 食欲をそそる／**personalized:** 個人的な／**relatively:** 比較的／**(make) on the spot:** すぐに作られる／**timeline:** 予定表／**take this and run with it:** これを引き継ぎ成功を目指して推し進める

3 Vocabulary Exercise

2 で確認した Vocabulary を使って、必要があれば変化形にした上で空欄を埋めてみよう。

(1) The music player wasn't very useful, so it was more of a _____.
(2) The high _____ laser is an important tool for the science lab.
(3) Engineers use great _____ with their designs, or else they won't work.
(4) It is difficult to _____ the weather, but computers do it well.
(5) There is nothing new about this _____ cooking technique.
(6) At first, smartphones were _____ as pointless, but now they are very common.
(7) Mix the flour, water, and yeast to make _____ for baking bread.
(8) Jo's kitchen was full of expensive and unique _____.

4 Topic Paragraph

ニュースの出だしの部分を確認し、下の［正誤］問題に答えてみよう。

AZUZ: And here's another one — 3D printer. They've been used to create everything from coat hangers and instruments, to cars and cups and clocks. And a number of engineers have been working to develop them as virtual chefs. This is easier to do for food that still has to be cooked afterwards, like breadsticks or ravioli, than something that's already hot and ready to eat. But a U.S. university has been experimenting with the cooking process in an effort to make 3D printed food something you can machine yourself at home.

True / False Questions

(1) 3D printers can be used to make cars.　　　　　　　　　　［ True / False ］
(2) It is more difficult to prepare uncooked food than hot food.　　［ True / False ］
(3) A U.S. university wants people to be able to make 3D printed food at home.
　　　　　　　　　　　　　　　　　　　　　　　　　　　　　　［ True / False ］

・・・・・・・・・・・・・・・・・ Try this! ・・・・・・・・・・・・・・・・・
1　リピーティング！　　2　オーバーラッピング！　　3　シャドーイング！

5 Memo

ノートなどに聞こえた単語やフレーズを書きながらニュースを聞いてみよう。

6 Transcript Completion

映像の音声や、ゆっくりと読み直した音声を聴いて空所に適切な語を入れてみよう。

AZUZ: And here's another one — 3D printer. They've been used to create everything from coat hangers and instruments, to cars and cups and clocks. And a number of engineers have been working to develop them as virtual chefs. This is easier to do for food that still has to be cooked afterwards, like breadsticks or ravioli, than something that's already hot and ready to eat. But a U.S. university has been experimenting with the cooking process in an effort to make 3D printed food something you can machine yourself at home.

UNIDENTIFIED MALE: If I try to imagine what your (1)_____ would look like in 10 years, you might have an extra appliance that it doesn't have today, and that would be a food printer, or maybe there'll be sexier name for it. But it (2)_____ you to do things you can't do today.

RACHEL CRANE, CNN CORRESPONDENT (voice-over): It's easy to dismiss 3D printing food as a novelty. But at Columbia's Creative Machines Lab, they're predicting that your future kitchen may have a 3D printer. Right now, what comes out of the machines isn't cooked. So, the team is trying to figure out the best way to cook food as it prints.

(on camera): Why do you need to incorporate lasers into 3D printing of food?

JONATHAN BLUTINGER, PHD CANDIDATE, MECHANICAL ENGINEERING: So, lasers offer you much higher resolution with cooking as opposed to conventional cooking methods like using an (3)_____. But a laser, it gives you that accuracy in the resolution and precision you need because now it's a pinpoint of (4)_____ that you can control where it goes.

CRANE: Ok. So, show me how this works. So, this guy is just browning the top.

BLUTINGER: And it only cooks about just under a millimeter of dough on the top. Which doesn't sound like a lot, but again, if you think about how these... how this will be used on a 3D food printer, you're only laying it out on a millimeter or two of food. So, you only really need to cook one to two millimeters.

CRANE (voice-over): It's the start of turning 3D food printing into a (5)_____ product.

(on camera): We're talking about, like, printing, like, goo?

HOD LIPSON, PROFESSOR OF MECHANICAL ENGINEERING, COLUMBIA: A lot of people have this kind of misconception that this is sort of Frankenstein food, right?

CRANE: Right. Doesn't seem so appetizing, Frankenstein food.

LIPSON: But the ingredients that you put into a food printer are (6)_____, water.

CRANE: It's kind of like, I mean, having your own chef in a way, that really knows everything that your body wants.

LIPSON: That's this magical (7)_____ of having sort of a personalized chef but also having it relatively low cost and made on the spot.

BLUTINGER: I think when I talked to people about food printing, the first thing is like, oh, you know, can we (8)_____ a (9)_____ or can we make, you know, some carrots? It's like, sure, you can do those things, but why would you want to do that when you have a machine that can pretty much make any combination of flavors?

CRANE: Right, something so much better than just, like, plain carrots. What timeline are we talking here? When do you think that this will actually be (10)_____ in people's kitchens? These lasers, these printers?

LIPSON: It's difficult to predict because it's more of a business question than of a technology. Technology is here. If a company wanted to take this and run with it, it could happen in a year.

7 Comprehension Questions

次の英文がニュースの内容に合っていればT (True)、合っていなければF (False) に丸印を付けよう。また、その根拠とした部分に下線を引いておこう。

Track 41

[T / F] (1)　The man thinks that people may have food printers in 10 years.

[T / F] (2)　Food printers might not be called "food printers" in the future.

[T / F] (3)　The Creative Machines Lab can already make cooked food.

Track 42

[T / F] (4)　They use ovens to cook the food in the printers.

[T / F] (5)　Conventional cooking methods are more accurate than lasers.

[T / F] (6)　Lasers cook the food on the top only.

Track 43

[T / F] (7)　The food printers make Frankenstein food.

[T / F] (8)　You can cook carrots using the printers.

[T / F] (9)　A lot more research must be done before the technology is ready.

8 Summary

次の文章はニュースの要約です。空所に適切な語を入れてみよう。

At Columbia's Creative Machines Lab, researchers are experimenting with 3D food printing technology. They (1.　　　　　) that in the kitchen of the future, we may all have an (2.　　　　　) based on this research. This idea has been (3.　　　　　) as something that is not useful, but it is not a (4.　　　　　). To cook (5.　　　　　) in the machine, scientists are using lasers because of their (6.　　　　　) and high (7.　　　　　). For this reason, lasers are better than using (8.　　　　　) ovens.

・・・・・・・・・・・・・・・・・・・ **Try this, too!** ・・・・・・・・・・・・・・・・・・・

ニュースの内容について、以下の質問をクラスメイトと話しあってみよう。

Discuss the good points and limits of 3D food printers. Make a poster / commercial for a 3D food printer.

Vocabulary / Idioms in the News
From Units 10-12

ここでは上記Unitに出てきた表現を特集して学習できます。

Exercise

左側の英単語・語句の意味を、右側の日本語訳と正しくつなげてみよう。

1.	a far cry from	( )	a.	いくつか例をあげると	
2.	Every dog has his day	( )	b.	連絡する	
3.	on alert	( )	c.	同一の	
4.	to name a few	( )	d.	どの犬にでも最高の時がある（誰にでも成功の機会はある）	
5.	been around	( )	e.	退けるのは簡単である	
6.	reach out to	( )	f.	存在している	
7.	one and the same	( )	g.	成功を目指して推し進める	
8.	easy to dismiss	( )	h.	～とは全く違って	
9.	as opposed to	( )	i.	～とは違って	
10.	run with it	( )	j.	注意深く見守って	

Unit 13 Bitcoin

ビットコインのオモテとウラ

未来型通貨として普及しつつあるビットコイン。でもその安全性は大丈夫なのでしょうか？最新の状況と問題点を見てみましょう。

1 Warm Up

(1) What is Bitcoin? Can you explain it in English?

(2) Have you ever used electronic currency? Why or why not?

(3) Do you think buying Bitcoin is dangerous? If yes, why?

2 Vocabulary

この課のニュースに出てくる重要単語の意味を選んでみよう。発音も確認してみよう。

49

1. fraud   (   )   5. redeemable   (   )
2. financial (   )   6. stuff   (   )
3. bankrupt   (   )   7. potentially   (   )
4. upswing   (   )   8. anonymously   (   )

a. 匿名で   e. 詐欺
b. 換金できる   f. 潜在的に
c. 上昇   g. 金融の
d. 破たんした   h. 物

Notes この課のニュースに出てくるやや難解な語（句）です。予め参考確認しておこう。

what's in: 流行っているもの／**institution:**（公共）機関／**agency:**（政府）機関／**whatsoever:** 全く／**PayPal:** ペイパル（インターネット決済サービスを提供する米国企業）／**regulator:** 監督機関／**representation:** 象徴／**run into some serious problems:** いくつかの深刻な問題に陥る／**exchange (like a money exchange):** 取引所／**MTGOX:** マウントゴックス（東京都拠点のビットコイン交換所）／**on top of that:** それに加えて／**surge:** 急騰する／**set a record:** 記録を打ち立てる／**factor in:** 要因となる／**JPMorgan:** JPモルガン（米国の投資銀行）／**hesitant:** 躊躇した

3 Vocabulary Exercise

2 で確認した Vocabulary を使って、必要があれば変化形にした上で空欄を埋めてみよう。

(1) The company's profits decreased so much last year that it went _____.
(2) Hiro posted on the Internet _____, so no one knows his name.
(3) She had too much _____ in her room, so she needed to clean it.
(4) Newspapers reported an _____ in the company's sales last month.
(5) Due to bank _____, many people lost all of their life savings.
(6) This water supply is _____ life saving if there's an earthquake.
(7) This gift card is _____ at any department store in town.
(8) Today's _____ reports look good for the future of the market.

4 Topic Paragraph

ニュースの出だしの部分を確認し、下の［正誤］問題に答えてみよう。

ZAIN ASHER, CNN MONEY: Using your credit card to buy stuff? That is so 20th century! Let me tell you what's in right now, ok? What's in right now is digital currency, so for example, Bitcoin. Now, Bitcoin completely lives online. It's sort of what makes it cool, but also what makes it potentially dangerous.

True / False Questions

(1) It is not cool to use a credit card to buy stuff.   [True / False]
(2) Digital currency is fashionable now.   [True / False]
(3) Bitcoin could be dangerous because it is online only.   [True / False]

• **Try this!** •

1 リピーティング！   2 オーバーラッピング！   3 シャドーイング！

5 Memo

ノートなどに聞こえた単語やフレーズを書きながらニュースを聞いてみよう。

Unit 13 Bitcoin

6 Transcript Completion

映像の音声や、ゆっくりと読み直した音声を聴いて空所に適切な語を入れてみよう。

ZAIN ASHER, CNN MONEY: Using your credit card to buy stuff? That is so 20th century! Let me tell you what's in right now, ok? What's in right now is digital currency, so for example, Bitcoin. Now, Bitcoin completely lives online. It's sort of what makes it cool, but also what makes it potentially dangerous.

OK. So, digital currency can be sent or received (1)_____ involving any financial institution or government agency whatsoever, OK? So, this is basically an online financial network that's completely open. There's no Visa, no PayPal, no regulators, right? So, it lives online, trades online and (2)_____ online. So, you're probably asking, OK, well, what about those golden bitcoins we've all seen? So, think of those like a gift card, OK? So, it's not (3)_____ money. It's just a sort of representation of money, only redeemable where bitcoins are accepted.

But, Bitcoin has actually already run into some serious problems. So, for example, one of the biggest exchanges out there, MTGOX, has already been shut down and is bankrupt. So, 1.75 million dollars worth of Bitcoin has literally just apparently (4)_____. But on top of that, the value of Bitcoin is constantly changing. So, one day, you might buy a bitcoin for, let's say, 500 dollars. The next day, the value could be (5)_____ of that. So, trust me when I tell you that this is very risky. But what's clear is, digital currency is the way of the future, but it's not (6)_____ certain if it's Bitcoin.

AZUZ: Bitcoin is on the upswing at the moment, though. A year ago, one unit would have cost you a little under (7)_____ dollars. Yesterday, that value had surged to more than (8)_____ dollars for one bitcoin. It set a record. Even financial analysts have had a hard time explaining Bitcoin's rises and falls. They think a couple of things may be factoring in here. One, it's possible that countries and companies that don't currently trade in Bitcoin will start doing it. And two, a (9)_____ form of the currency was created earlier this year and that might have made investors more confident in it. Some analysts don't expect Bitcoin to stay this valuable, though. The head of JP Morgan, an investment company, has called it a fraud. And experts believe that governments will be hesitant to allow large payments to be made anonymously with Bitcoin, because it would be harder to stop (10)_____ and collect (11)_____.

7 Comprehension Questions

次の英文がニュースの内容に合っていればT (True)、合っていなければF (False) に丸印を付けよう。また、その根拠とした部分に下線を引いておこう。

Track 53

[T / F] (1) Bitcoin is controlled by a government agency.
[T / F] (2) According to the text, many people have seen golden bitcoins.
[T / F] (3) Golden bitcoins cannot be used to pay for anything.

Track 54

[T / F] (4) You can trade Bitcoin on MTGOX.
[T / F] (5) The value of Bitcoin is going up continually.
[T / F] (6) Zain thinks that Bitcoin might not be successful.

Track 55

[T / F] (7) The value of Bitcoin was going up at the time of the report.
[T / F] (8) It's easy to understand Bitcoin's changing value.
[T / F] (9) Not everybody thinks that Bitcoin is a good thing.

8 Summary

次の文章はニュースの要約です。空所に適切な語を入れてみよう。

Bitcoin is a digital currency which can be used to buy (1.   ). Though we sometimes see real golden bitcoins, these are only (2.   ) in certain places. The currency is not regulated by any (3.   ) institution, so money can be used (4.   ). This means that Bitcoin could (5.   ) be used by criminals to avoid taxes or commit (6.   ). The value of the currency is changing quickly. One exchange dealing in Bitcoin is already (7.   ), but the currency is on the (8.   ) at the moment.

• **Try this, too!** •

ニュースの内容について、以下の質問をクラスメイトと話しあってみよう。

Discuss the advantages and disadvantages of Bitcoin. When you give your opinion, you have to show at least one piece of evidence to support your opinion.

Unit 14 Money to Soil

古くなった紙幣は土へ

古くなって使い物にならなくなった紙幣はどうなるのでしょうか？リサイクルに回り、土へと変化しているアメリカの例を見てみましょう。

1 Warm Up

(1) Have you ever had old, worn out money?

(2) What kinds of recycling do you know?

(3) Are you interested in agriculture? If you have a chance, what would you like to grow?

2 Vocabulary

この課のニュースに出てくる重要単語の意味を選んでみよう。発音も確認してみよう。

1. fulfilling (　)　　5. shred (　)
2. landfill (　)　　6. trillion (　)
3. trash (　)　　7. ensure (　)
4. compost (　)　　8. circulation (　)

a. 兆	e. 確実にする
b. 細断する	f. ゴミ廃棄場
c. やりがいがある	g. 堆肥
d. 流通	h. ゴミ

Notes この課のニュースに出てくるやや難解な語（句）です。予め参考確認しておこう。

the Federal Reserve Bank: 連邦準備銀行／**regardless:** 〜に関わらず／**enrich:** 肥沃にする／**cash:** 現金／**lead business analyst:** 主任ビジネス分析家／**unfit:** 不適格な／**rip:** 裂け目／**graffiti:** 落書き／**wind up as:** 結局〜になる／**ultimately:** 究極的に／**facility:** 施設／**deem:** 見なす／**urban:** 都市の／**accessible:** 入手しやすい／**veggie:** 野菜／**cucumber:** きゅうり

3 Vocabulary Exercise

2 で確認した Vocabulary を使って、必要があれば変化形にした上で空欄を埋めてみよう。

(1) To make _____, mix food scraps and dirt in a pile.

(2) These papers contain personal information, so please _____ them.

(3) The _____ of the newspaper has decreased for the last two decades.

(4) Things you throw away are either burned or taken to a _____.

(5) To _____ safety, it is necessary to wear a helmet at all times.

(6) Peter loved his job and thought it was very _____.

(7) Nanako put the plastic wrap and paper scraps in the _____.

(8) There are about one _____ stars in our galaxy alone.

4 Topic Paragraph

ニュースの出だしの部分を確認し、下の［正誤］問題に答えてみよう。

AZUZ: From dead stars to dead money. According to the U.S. Federal Reserve, about 1.53 trillion worth of U.S. bills are in circulation right now. But regardless of when exactly they were printed, these bills at some point have to come out of circulation, and some of them are used to enrich the soil. That's today's "Great Big Story."

True / False Questions

(1) 1.53 million dollars of currency was in circulation at that time.　　[True / False]

(2) The bills can be used forever.　　[True / False]

(3) Soil can be made better by using money.　　[True / False]

• Try this! •

1　リピーティング！　　2　オーバーラッピング！　　3　シャドーイング！

5 Memo

ノートなどに聞こえた単語やフレーズを書きながらニュースを聞いてみよう。

6 Transcript Completion

映像の音声や、ゆっくりと読み直した音声を聴いて空所に適切な語を入れてみよう。

AZUZ: From dead stars to dead money. According to the U.S. Federal Reserve, about 1.53 trillion worth of U.S. bills are in circulation right now. But regardless of when exactly they were printed, these bills at some point have to come out of circulation, and some of them are used to enrich the soil. That's today's "Great Big Story."

REPORTER: Money, it's everywhere. But what happens when your bills get old and need to be replaced by new ones? That means old cash needs to be (1)_____—a lot of cash. This is not, however, the story of money growing on trees, but of trees growing out of money. Well, more like (2)_____.

DEAN WOITHA, LEAD BUSINESS ANALYST, NEW ORLEANS FED: We are here at the Federal Reserve Bank in New Orleans and this is where we shred millions of dollars. My name is Dean Woitha. I'm the lead business analyst for cash services here at the New Orleans Fed. We are the nation's bank. Our job is to make sure that we have a (3)_____ of currency. Also part of that is to ensure that we remove unfit, old dirty currency from circulation.

So, here on (4)_____, we shred about $6 million in dirty money every day. This could be for any number of reasons. It could be because the note has rips in it, holes in it, tears in it. It could have (5)_____ on it. It could have graffiti written all over it. We don't want that note going back into circulation. If it has any sort of those qualities, it will be shredded. What we used to do is take all of these currency shreds, and they would just wind up as waste going to a landfill. Now, through a lot of work and effort, we finally figured out a way where we can take these shreds and ultimately recycle them.

REPORTER: So, all that green leaves the Fed and heads to a compost facility, where it turns into something quite useful.

JOHNATHAN CHRISTIAN STROUD, DIRCTOR, WOOD MATERIALS LLC: What you're looking at right now is (6)_____ million dollars. But the soil that it creates will be (7)_____. My name is Jonathan Christian. We turn cash into soil. It is definitely one of our secret ingredients. It's little in content but it's huge in what it provides. Currency that's deemed unfit is brought to our facility at Wood Materials. From there, we go through a simple composting process where we convert that into a (8)_____ soil. Our compost is used primarily by urban farmers in the greater New Orleans area.

REPORTER: One of these farmers is Simond Menasche.

SIMOND MENASCHE, FOUNDER & DIRECTOR, GROW ON: And this is a million dollar farm. We are making fresh local food accessible in New Orleans. We've grown veggies, herbs, cucumbers, tomatoes, and peppers. The vegetables we grow here are made out of compost and cash. It is very fulfilling to be growing using a material that would (9)_____ go to waste. One man's trash is another man's treasure.

REPORTER: And that's the story of how we grow (10)_____ out of cash.

7 Comprehension Questions

次の英文がニュースの内容に合っていればT (True)、合っていなければF (False) に丸印を付けよう。また、その根拠とした部分に下線を引いておこう。

Track 65

[T / F] (1) When bills get old, they have to be destroyed.
[T / F] (2) Money is not shredded in New Orleans.
[T / F] (3) The New Orleans Fed is responsible for the circulation of money.

Track 66

[T / F] (4) If a note has things written all over it, then it is destroyed.
[T / F] (5) The bills used to be shredded and turned into compost.
[T / F] (6) Now the shredded notes are put into a landfill.

Track 67

[T / F] (7) Jonathan thinks the money is important to make good soil.
[T / F] (8) A lot of the compost made by Wood Materials is used outside New Orleans.
[T / F] (9) Simond grows vegetables using compost with money in it.

8 Summary

次の文章はニュースの要約です。空所に適切な語を入れてみよう。

One of the jobs of the Federal Reserve Bank is to (1.   ) that when money gets old, it is (2.   ). In the past, that paper (3.   ) would then be thrown away into a (4.   ). Now, however, when those bills get too old, they are used to make (5.   ), some of which is then used to grow fruit and vegetables. Simon Menasche is a farmer who finds it (6.   ) to turn some of the waste, created by the (7.   ) of dollars worth of bills that are in (8.   ), into something useful.

• **Try this, too!** •

ニュースの内容について、以下の質問をクラスメイトと話しあってみよう。

Are Japanese bills recycled in the same way as in the U.S.? Research this topic and tell your classmates about your results.

Unit 15 Net Neutrality

ネットワーク中立性を考えよう

アメリカにはネットワーク中立性という考え方があります。その是非について考えてみましょう。

1 Warm Up

(1) How much time do you spend on the Internet every day?

(2) Do you think Internet companies should be able to charge a lot of money?

(3) Do you think the Internet should be free from rules (laws)?

2 Vocabulary

この課のニュースに出てくる重要単語の意味を選んでみよう。発音も確認してみよう。

1. repeal   ( )   5. utility   ( )
2. prioritize   ( )   6. perspective   ( )
3. infrastructure ( )   7. deregulation   ( )
4. entrepreneur   ( )   8. thrive   ( )

a. 企業家	e. 規則撤廃
b. 廃止する	f. 成功する
c. 施設	g. 今後の見通し
d. インフラ（社会的基盤）	h. 優先する

Notes この課のニュースに出てくるやや難解な語（句）です。予め参考確認しておこう。

the U.S. Federal Communications Commission: 米国連邦通信委員会／**take effect:** 有効になる／**Comcast** コムキャスト（米国ケーブルテレビ企業）／**Verizon:** ベライゾン（米国大手電気通信事業者）／**tenet:** 原則／**AT&T:**（米国最大手の電話会社）／**be put in place:** 導入される／**unleash:** 解放する／**innovator:** 革新者／**regulatory inertia:** 規則の惰性／**get ~ out of ...:** ～に…をやめさせる／**micromanage:** 細かく管理する／**earn the praise of:** ～の賞賛を得る／**on the other side of the coin:** その反面に／**consumer advocacy groups:** 消費者擁護団体／**open question:** 未解決の問題

3 Vocabulary Exercise

2 で確認した Vocabulary を使って、必要があれば変化形にした上で空欄を埋めてみよう。

(1) The small town had only basic _____: electric power and sewage.

(2) After _____, a private company controlled the town's water.

(3) The vegetables grew in rich and healthy soil, so they _____.

(4) Roads and bridges are part of a country's _____.

(5) The manager had a lot of work, so he _____ the important things.

(6) The government _____ the speed limit law, so now we can drive faster.

(7) From a child's _____, one year is a very long period of time.

(8) George is an _____ and often starts new businesses.

4 Topic Paragraph

ニュースの出だしの部分を確認し、下の［正誤］問題に答えてみよう。

AZUZ: The U.S. Federal Communications Commission voted yesterday to relax the government's rules concerning net neutrality. The vote was 3 to 2, with three Republicans voting to repeal the rules, and two Democrats voting to keep them in place. The repeal won't take effect immediately — that should happen sometime next year — and what it means is that Internet service providers like Comcast and Verizon will no longer be prevented from speeding up or slowing down Internet traffic from specific websites or applications. They'll also be allowed to prioritize their own content. But if they do any of this, they'll have to show publicly that they did and then the government will decide whether it's fair or not. Perspective on whether this is a good or bad thing depends on whom you talk to.

True / False Questions

(1) The Republicans want to relax the rules about net neutrality.　［ True / False ］

(2) Internet service providers will be able to change the speed of Internet traffic.

　　　　　　　　　　　　　　　　　　　　　　　　　　　　　　　　　［ True / False ］

(3) The public will judge if prioritizing content is fair.　［ True / False ］

• Try this! •

1 リピーティング！　　**2** オーバーラッピング！　　**3** シャドーイング！

CNN 10, Vol. 2 – Student News –

5 Memo

ノートなどに聞こえた単語やフレーズを書きながらニュースを聞いてみよう。

6 Transcript Completion

映像の音声や、ゆっくりと読み直した音声を聴いて空所に適切な語を入れてみよう。

AZUZ: The U.S. Federal Communications Commission voted yesterday to relax the government's rules concerning net neutrality. The vote was 3 to 2, with three Republicans voting to repeal the rules, and two Democrats voting to keep them in place. The repeal won't take effect immediately — that should happen sometime next year — and what it means is that Internet service providers like Comcast and Verizon will no longer be prevented from speeding up or slowing down Internet traffic from specific websites or applications. They'll also be allowed to prioritize their own content. But if they do any of this, they'll have to show publicly that they did and then the government will decide whether it's fair or not. Perspective on whether this is a good or bad thing depends on whom you talk to.

JON SARLIN, CNNMONEY PRODUCER: If the Internet is a highway, (1)_____, or content providers, can't pay more to use a special fast lane. Think of it this way: all content is created equal in the eyes of the Internet provider. That's the basic tenet (2)_____ net neutrality. So, if the Internet is neutral, then the Internet providers are treated basically like public utilities. Comcast or AT&T, they couldn't slow down or speed up certain content. But if net neutrality ends, some companies are going to be stuck in that slow lane. The (3)_____ that made the Net neutral were put in place during the Obama administration.

BARACK OBAMA, FORMER PRESIDENT: This set of principles, the idea of net neutrality, has unleashed the power of the Internet and given innovators the (4)_____ to thrive.

SARLIN: But now, things are going in a different direction. Ajit Pai is now the chairman of the FCC. He's a (5)_____ (6)_____ for Verizon.

AJIT PAI, FCC CHAIRMAN: Entrepreneurs are constantly developing new technologies and services, but too often, they're unable to bring them to market for consumers because outdated rules or regulatory inertia (7)_____ in the way.

SARLIN: To him, repealing net neutrality will lead to innovation, that will get the government out of micromanaging the Internet. The Internet providers will have more money, they'll then (8)_____ more in infrastructure, and we'll have faster streaming. But while deregulation certainly has earned the praise of the telecommunications industry, on the other side of the coin, you have tech companies and consumer advocacy groups. The open question now: will repeal of net neutrality lead to innovation or to a (9)_____ (10)_____?

7 Comprehension Questions

次の英文がニュースの内容に合っていればT (True)、合っていなければF (False) に丸印を付けよう。また、その根拠とした部分に下線を引いておこう。

Track 77

[T / F] (1) Net neutrality means that there is a fast lane for some content.
[T / F] (2) Internet providers like Comcast are public utilities.
[T / F] (3) When Obama was president, the Internet was made neutral.

Track 78

[T / F] (4) Obama supported the idea of net neutrality.
[T / F] (5) The chairman of the FCC wants to make the Net more neutral.
[T / F] (6) Ajit Pai thinks new technology cannot be sold because of old laws.

Track 79

[T / F] (7) More innovation may be the result of repealing net neutrality.
[T / F] (8) Internet providers will make money out of deregulation.
[T / F] (9) Tech companies are generally against net neutrality.

8 Summary

次の文章はニュースの要約です。空所に適切な語を入れてみよう。

The U.S. government has (1.) the rules concerning net neutrality. This means that the telecom industry will be able to (2.) access to certain sites and applications. In the past, firms like Comcast and AT&T were similar to government (3.) in the way they were treated. Different people have different (4.) on this (5.). Some people believe that with a change in the rules, (6.) will be able to (7.) and the telecom industry will have the opportunity to build better (8.) and improve internet speeds.

•••••••••••••••••••• **Try this, too!** ••••••••••••••••••••

ニュースの内容について、以下の質問をクラスメイトと話しあってみよう。

Discuss the advantages or disadvantages of net neutrality. When you give your opinion, you have to show at least one piece of evidence to support your opinion.

Vocabulary / Idioms in the News
From Units 13-15

ここでは上記 Unit に出てきた表現を特集して学習できます。

Exercise

左側の英単語・語句の意味を、右側の日本語訳と正しくつなげてみよう。

1.	what's in right now	( )	a.	問題に陥る
2.	sort of	( )	b.	市場に持ち込む
3.	on the upswing	( )	c.	〜に向かう
4.	run into problems	( )	d.	お金は木に生らない
5.	regardless of	( )	e.	現在流行しているもの
6.	head to	( )	f.	途中に立ちはだかる
7.	money doesn't grow on trees	( )	g.	いわば
8.	wind up as	( )	h.	〜に関わらず
9.	brought to market	( )	i.	〜になる
10.	stand in the way	( )	j.	上昇している

CNN 10 Vol. 2
― Student News ―

検印省略

©2019 年 1 月 31 日 初版発行

著者 関戸冬彦
　　　小暮正人
　　　Jake Arnold
　　　Christopher Mattson
　　　長 和重

発行者 原 雅久

発行所 株式会社朝日出版社
　　　101-0065 東京都千代田区西神田 3-3-5
　　　電話 (03) 3239-0271
　　　FAX (03) 3239-0479
　　　e-mail: text-e@asahipress.com
　　　組版・ファースト／製版・信毎書籍印刷

乱丁, 落丁本はお取り替えいたします。
ISBN978-4-255-15633-0

最高クオリティの問題と解説により
圧倒的な効率でスコアUP!

韓国TOEIC運営企業YBM社が30年間のノウハウで頻出形式を徹底的に分析!

YBM TOEIC 研究所=著　　各本体3,400円+税　B5判変型

韓国TOEIC運営企業の究極の模試×10回分

TOEIC® L&Rテスト YBM超実戦模試 リスニング1000問

TOEIC® L&Rテスト YBM超実戦模試 リーディング1000問

リスニング
460ページ(本冊168頁、別冊292頁)

MP3音声CD-ROM＋3パターンの音声ダウンロード付き

▶付属CD-ROMに通常音声を収録。
▶ダウンロードでは通常音声のほか
　〈1.2倍速音声〉
　〈本番環境に近い雑音入り音声〉
　も提供。

リーディング
528ページ(本冊336頁、別冊192頁)

朝日出版社　〒101-0065 東京都千代田区西神田 3-3-5　TEL 03-3263-3321

生きた英語でリスニング!

1本30秒だから、聞きやすい!

CNN ニュース・リスニング
2018［秋冬］
生声CD・対訳付き・A5判　本体1000円+税

世界標準の英語ニュースがだれでも
聞き取れるようになる［30秒×3回聞き］方式!
- 大坂なおみ、全米オープン優勝の快挙!
- 「ゲーム障害」をWHOが病気と認定
- レディー・ガガ、反性暴力の声を上げる...など

スティーブ・ジョブズ
伝説のスピーチ&プレゼン
- 伝説のスタンフォード大学スピーチ
- 驚異のプレゼンでたどるジョブズの軌跡
- 伝記本の著者が明かすカリスマの素顔
- CNNが振り返るジョブズの功績

生声CD・対訳付き・A5判
本体1000円+税

スタンフォードの
「英語ができる自分」になる教室
ケリー・マクゴニガル　生声CD・対訳付き・A5判　本体1000円+税

意識が変われば英語力はぐんぐん伸びる! 英語をモノにする意志力の鍛え方、
「なりたい自分」になるための戦略...など、だれも教えてくれなかった「学習のひみつ」を
スタンフォード大学人気講師が解き明かす。

セレブたちの卒業式スピーチ
次世代に贈る言葉　生声CD・対訳付き・A5判　本体1200円+税

アメリカ名門大学で語られた未来を担う者たちへのメッセージ
- ビル&メリンダ・ゲイツ
- メリル・ストリープ［女優］
- ティム・クック［アップルCEO］
- アーノルド・シュワルツェネッガー
- イーロン・マスク［テスラモーターズCEO］

朝日出版社　〒101-0065 東京都千代田区西神田 3-3-5　TEL 03-3263-3321